Prayer Life

VOLUME 1

TRACY L. WILLIAMS

Prayer Life

...FOR KINGS IN THE KINGDOM OF GOD

TLW PUBLICATIONS

Published by TLW Publications
P.O. Box 1413
Claremont, CA 91711 - 1413

First edition print January 2015

Printed in the United States of America

ISBN: 978-0-9894241-1-0 (Hardcover)
ISBN: 978-0-9894241-2-7 (ebook / ePub)
ISBN: 978-0-9894241-3-4 (ebook / Mobi & Kindle)

Photo credits: Roman soldier, DollarPhotoClub © GooDAura; goldren scepter, DollarPhotoClub © Yexela and Pixelrobot, background (digital orange waves): DollarPhotoClub © Tupungato; background (leather texture), RDStudio; flying dove, DollarPhotoClub © Fotomaster; goldren royal crown, DollarPhotoClub © Oleksiy Mark; female warrior: (body) DollarPhotoClub © Gordana Sermek and (face) DollarPhotoClub © Paul Hill. Photo-manipulation by RD Studio.

Book design by DesignForBooks.com

DEDICATION

I dedicate this faith project to the
Holy Spirit—my Helper, Comforter, Strengthener,
Standby, Advocate, Counselor, and Intercessor.

Thank You, Father God for sending the Holy Spirit.

Thank You, Lord Jesus for praying forth the Holy Spirit.

Thank You, Holy Spirit for coming.

I love YOU.

CONTENTS

Forward XI
Introduction—The Author's Heart XIII

1. Peace With God 1

Prayer to Get Born Again 2
Prayer For Backsliders to Return 4
Prayer to Receive the Gift of the Holy Spirit 6
Release from Any Stronghold of Guilt 8

2. Prophetic Words for kings Edification 11

"I Am a King!"—10 Reminders of Your Kingship 12
Reminder of God Given Purpose 16
"Who I Am" 18
"Stay Where You Are—You Are Being Prepared" 21
A Prophet's Prayer 23

PART ONE

HOW A KING STARTS THE DAY FOR VICTORY

3. A kings Ministry to the Lord 27

Worship to The King of kings & The Lord of lords 28
My Soul Thirsts for More of You Lord 30
My Soul Waits for You, God, and Expects From You Only 32
Kings Rise Early to Pray 34

The Blessing of Divine Protection 36
Rebuking an Evil Day While Continuing to Stand 39
A king's Desire for The Father's Will to Be Done 41
Receiving All That Heaven Has for the Day 43
Anxiety and Worry Free! 44
Every king Pleads the Blood of Jesus 46

PART TWO

PRAYERS FOR KINGS ANYTIME OF DAY OR NIGHT

4. The kings Call to Minister Reconciliation 51

Prayer to Receive the Gift of the Holy Spirit 52
Receive Anointing to Witness as Mandated 54
A king Mindful of Heaven's Vision 57
Confidence to Minister 59
Daily Intercession for Your Fruit to Remain 61
Prayer Over Spiritual Children (Disciples) 63
We All Have a Ministry 65

5. The kings Call to Intercession 67

Calling in Lost Souls 68
Prayer for Spiritual Wisdom and Understanding 70
Plead The Blood of Jesus Over the Church 72
Prayer for Missions Overseas 74
Binding Whisperers 77

6. Personal Ministry Related (For Male or Female kings) 79

Every king Has a Sound Mind—No Fear 80

Kingdom Benefits for All kings 82
kings Put Off the Old 84
A king Depriving Their Flesh of Power 86
A king with a Pure Heart 88
A king's Desire to Please God and Not Men 90
A king Increasing in the Nature of Love 101A 92
A king Increasing in the Nature of Love 101B 95
A king Increasing in the Nature of Love 101C 97
No Longer a Child but a Son of God 99
A king of No Compromise 101
A king's Fruitful Growth in Faith 103
A king's Quest for Wisdom—*Only* 105
The Anointing to Complete 107
Increase in the Ability to Discern Spirits 109
Overcome Arrogance and Walk in Humility 111
Receive Kingdom Mysteries Revealed 113
For Men Specifically:
  Victory Over Kingship Removers 115
For Women Specifically:
  Healing for Hurting Women—Abused by Words 118
  Taming a Tongue on Fire 120
  A Woman Confronting Their Mind 122
  A Woman Free From the World's System 124
  I Am a Virtuous Woman! 126
For Divine Health:
  God's Medicine for Long Life 128
  Living The Lifestyle of the Healed 130
For The king's Family:
  The Devil's Campaign Against Marriages *Cancelled!* 132

A king's Prophetic Prayer Over His/Her Children 135
Spiritual Dominion for Parents of an Adopted Child 140
For Finances:
Rebuke Mighty Nations That Hinders Prosperity 142
Poverty Will No Longer Find Me 144
A Promise for Seed Sowers 147
Supernatural Debt Cancellation 151
The Blessings of Obedience 153
A king's Enemies Defeated 156

7. Corporate Ministry Related (For Intercessors of a Ministry) 159

Worship Service Opening Prayer 160
Pre-Service Warfare Victory 162
Binding of Mockers and Scorners 168
Prayer Before Corporate/Community Outreach 169
Prayer After Corporate/Community Outreach 175
Taking Possession of Land Promised 179
Declaration of Budget Met 182

8. Quick "On The Go" Power Confessions for kings 185

Contact Page 196

FOREWORD

Prayer Life, by Tracy L. Williams, is a very inspiring book. This book contains prayers that one can pray for any situation, challenge, or need that they may find themselves in. Tracy has spent many hours studying God's word and continued intercession for the body of Christ. She refers to us as kings in the kingdom of God. And as kings we have privileges. She has written prayers concerning salvation, how to receive the Holy Spirit, and rededicating one's life to Christ. She also shares on praise and worship to our Lord.

Tracy speaks about love and faith in receiving from God. As a result of our faith, we can have the finances; good marriages; freedom from worry; help in ministry; help for hurting women; wisdom for men to help them stay out of trouble; healing; and you name it.

I believe that you will be blessed and helped as you take time to read, meditate on, and pray these prayers.

Betty R. Price, D.D.
Crenshaw Christian Center

INTRODUCTION

The Author's Heart

Do not fret or have any anxiety about anything, but in every circumstance and in everything, by PRAYER and petition (definite requests), with thanksgiving, continue to make your wants known to God. And God's peace (shall be yours, that tranquil state of a soul assured of its salvation through Christ, and so fearing nothing from God and being content with its earthly lot of whatever sort that is, that peace) which transcends all understanding shall garrison and mount guard over your hearts and minds in Christ Jesus. For the rest, brethren, whatever is true, whatever is worthy of reverence and is honorable and seemly, whatever is just, whatever is pure, whatever is lovely and lovable, whatever is kind and winsome and gracious, if there is any virtue and excellence, if there is anything worthy of praise, think on and weigh and take account of these things (fix your minds on them). Practice what you have learned and received and heard and seen in me, and model your way of living on it, and the God of peace (of untroubled, undisturbed well-being) will be with you.

~ *PHILIPPIANS 4:6–9 AMP*

Every believer is a king in the kingdom of God regardless of gender. We all have a prophetic voice that, once released (empowered by the word of God) causes promises to be made real and experienced. I believe that once we confess God's word from our own mouths our faith is increased, and as we listen with a spiritual ear to what we are releasing—*not just saying a prayer*, but declaring the word of God **boldly** as we ought to—we will believe what we have spoken and we will expect great, quick results. This not only promotes confidence and boldness in our lives to live as kings here in the earth realm, but it is faith that moves God to act on our behalf, while mountains are being removed and our destiny lined up with God's perfect will for our lives. It's the courage to deal head on with whatever may be in our way.

The antichrist is here . . .

. . . currently trying to come against the believer in every area of our lives. Coming against our relationships with God, our relationships with our spouses, our relationships with our children, our relationships with our families and friends, and our relationships in our local ministries of the gospel. As men and women of faith we must stand against the strategies of the enemy by speaking, declaring, praying, and confessing the word of God.

Just as Jesus, when tempted in the book of Matthew chapter four, also spoke the word of God. I know that out of all the works of the enemy, the ultimate work he has put into effect is the attempt to draw kings (us) back from the faith that has been given to us "once and for all."

> "But the just shall live by faith (My righteous servant shall live by his conviction, respecting man's relationship to God and divine things, and holy fervor born of faith and conjoined with it); and if he draws back and shrinks in fear, My soul has no delight or pleasure in him."
>
> ~ *Hebrews 10:38 AMP*

> "(Motivated) by faith he (Moses) left Egypt behind him, being unawed and undismayed by the wrath of the king; for he never flinched but held staunchly to his purpose, and endured steadfastly as one who gazed on Him Who is invisible."
>
> ~ *Hebrews 11:27 AMP*

> "When Pharaoh heard of it, he sought to slay Moses. But Moses fled from Pharaoh's presence and took refuge in the land of Midian, where he sat down by the well."
>
> ~ *Exodus 2:15 AMP*

Jesus spoke the word of God when the enemy was trying to come against Him. Moses fled the very presence of evil by taking refuge and sitting by a well. The word of God is the well of life that we must speak from our hearts and through our mouths to cause the enemy to flee immediately as we continue to stand in faith—not being moved.

Now is not the time to be moved.

As we are reminded in 2 Corinthians 10:3–4 and Ephesians 6:12, we are not warring against flesh and blood (people) but against principalities and rulers of darkness in this age. At times we are even battling against the old thoughts and nature of our natural mind that resists the very help and wisdom of God. This type of battling must come into divine order as we release it through prayer and confessions centered in specific areas of warfare. We must lean on, trust in, take refuge in, and speak the word of God by faith—boldly.

In this first volume of bold confessions you will find a compilation of works revealed during my own personal time spent with the Lord. As the Lord would place it upon my heart to birth a specific prayer through His word, or if I was given an assignment by my Pastor, I would immediately consult with the Holy Spirit as He would lead me and guide me to the exact scriptures that would serve as key and foundational verses that would complete the prayer or confession. Some are prophetic words that will stir up your faith immediately meeting you right where you are—as they have done the same for me.

I know these prayers are for right now.

I know they will meet the need of whoever chooses to implement them in their daily prayer life—as led to do so by the Spirit of God. Some of these prayers you will read only one time and then from there simply thank God for the manifestation of your prayer released. Others, you may read daily as you travail, stand, and endure in a specific area until you actually see—with your physical eyes the promised victory. Ultimately, these prayers will be used as a source of intercession for others.

Whatever the case may be or wherever the level of your faith may be, I pray that this first volume of "Right Now" prayers and "Confessions for kings" will serve you and those in the sphere of your influence in a great way. A great way, that will prove how faithful God is to His word and how key our obedience is to act in faith as we put action to our words spoken. This will bring expected victory in every area of your life and in the lives of others—as applied when needed.

Remember, you are a king if you have entered into the kingdom of God, and you have the right to peace, love, joy, righteousness, and the Holy Spirit. Jesus is the King of kings and the Lord of lords. You are a king in His Kingdom and you have rights and benefits that should be experienced right here, right now. It's time that you took your rightful place "like never before" and begin to speak as your Father would have you to—boldly displacing all works of darkness, disconnection, and discomfort.

Co-laboring with Christ,

Tracy L. Williams

Always transparent, real, willing and obedient to
share when advised from above to do so ☺.

CHAPTER

PEACE WITH GOD

Do you have peace in your heart concerning God? If not, this chapter will present you the opportunity to make peace with God through your confession and to receive His divine grace—His favor upon your life. Come humbly understanding that you did not choose Him, but by His grace He chose you. Also, if you stepped away from the faith you once received, come back. For anyone reading this you can have a fresh start today.

> Therefore, since we are justified (acquitted, declared righteous, and given a right standing with God) through faith, let us [grasp the fact that we] have [the peace of reconciliation to hold and to enjoy] peace with God through our Lord Jesus Christ (the Messiah, the Anointed One).
>
> ~ *Romans 5:1*

PRAYER TO GET BORN AGAIN

To Enter into the Kingdom of God as a king for the First Time

"From that time Jesus began to preach and to say, Repent, for the kingdom of heaven is at hand."

~ *Matthew 4:17 NKJV*

Father God,

I come to You just as I am.

Live in me and through me.

I know in my heart, and I confess with my mouth, that Jesus Christ was raised from the dead, and is now seated at Your right hand in Heaven.

I repent and I acknowledge that I was a sinner. But now, by my confession of faith, by Your grace God, and by the precious blood of Jesus, I am saved. I am born again, in Jesus' name.

I receive my new life in Christ—eternal life—and Jesus is my Lord and my Savoir.

Thank You . . . I say "Abba, Father", in Jesus' name.

So be it. Amen.

> "Likewise, I say to you, there is joy in the presence of the angels of God over one sinner who repents."
>
> ~*Luke 15:10 NKJV*

Romans 8:15
Romans 10:8, 9
Matthew 4:17
Luke 15:10
Colossians 1:14

PRAYER FOR BACKSLIDERS TO RETURN

"Return, you backsliding children, and I will heal your backslidings." "Indeed we do come to You, for You are the Lord our God."

~*Jeremiah 3:22*

Father God, forgive me for drawing back from the faith that you have given me. I repent in Jesus' name and I renew my vow to love You with all my heart, soul, mind, and strength.

I thank You, Father, for forgiving me and forgetting my mistakes. I am born of God and I sin not. Your word reminds me in Isaiah 43:25, "I, even I, am He who blots out and cancels your transgressions, for My own sake, and I will not remember your sins."

I take my authority and I curse at the root any residuals of a backslider in my heart and the dictates of my own ways. I declare that I am satisfied from above. I am not the simple who believes every word, but I am the prudent who considers well my every step. (Proverbs 14:14–15) I am not like a dog who returns to his vomit nor like the fool who repeats his foolishness. (Proverbs 26:11 NLT)

I believe I receive my prayer of faith. I forgive myself and I move forward. I'm determined to further understanding and be serious about the salvation and life that I've received.

This is my hour and time to truly be enlightened and experience the good things of heaven and share in The Holy Spirit. I will taste the goodness of the word of God and the power of the age to come (Hebrews 6:3–6).

Thank You for Your love and the power to remind You of Your word. Your promise to me of eternal life—through my Lord and Savior Jesus.

> "I will heal their backsliding, I will love them freely, for My anger has turned away from him."
>
> ~ *Hosea 14:4*

PRAYER TO RECEIVE THE GIFT OF THE HOLY SPIRIT

"And he asked them, 'Did you receive the Holy Spirit when you believed (on Jesus as the Christ)?' And they said, 'No, we have not even heard that there is a Holy Spirit.'"

~ *Acts 19:2*

"... how much more shall your heavenly Father give the Holy Spirit to them that ask Him?"

~ *Luke 11:13 KJV*

"For the promise (of the Holy Spirit) is to and for you and your children, and to and for all that are far away, (even) to and for as many as the Lord our God invites and bids to come to Himself."

~ *Acts 2:39*

"But you shall receive power (ability, efficiency, and might) when the Holy Spirit has come upon you, and you shall be My witnesses . . ."

~ *Acts 1:8*

> "And whatever you ask for in prayer, having faith and (really) believing . . . , you will receive."
>
> ~ *Matthew 21:22*

Heavenly Father,

As Your child, I ask for and I receive the gift of the Holy Spirit by faith!

I receive the baptism and infilling of the Holy Spirit.

I receive the Holy Spirit's power to witness and operate in the fruit of the Spirit.

I receive evidence of speaking in another tongue—the language of my heart where the Holy Spirit lives.

Holy Spirit, take charge of my tongue as I yield my tongue to Your use.

I receive utterance right now! I receive tongues of fire right now!

I am born again and I am spirit-filled with the evidence of speaking in another tongue! In Jesus' name, so be it—Amen.

*Now open your mouth and give it a sound. You are in control. You can start and stop praying in the Spirit at anytime.

> "Therefore, brethren, desire earnestly to prophesy, and do not forbid to speak with tongues."
>
> ~ *1 Corinthians 14:39 NKJV*

Acts 19:2
Acts 1:8
Luke 11:13

RELEASE FROM ANY STRONGHOLD OF GUILT

By this we shall come to know (perceive, recognize, and understand) that we are of the Truth, and can reassure (quiet, conciliate, and pacify) our hearts in His presence, whenever our hearts in (tormenting) self-accusation make us feel guilty and condemn us. (For we are in God's hands.) For He is above and greater than our conscience (our hearts), and He knows (perceives and understands) everything (nothing is hidden from Him).

~ *I JOHN 3:19–20*

By faith, I rebuke the spirit of condemnation. I am in Christ Jesus. There is no condemnation, no guilt, or wrong in me. I have a contrite heart that is quick to repent, and I know that I have been forgiven.

I live and I walk not after the dictates of my flesh, but after the dictates of the Holy Spirit. The law of the Spirit of life in Christ Jesus—the law of my new being—has freed me from the law of sin and of death. I have been cleansed by The Word of God that abides in me and by the blood of Jesus.

I rebuke any spirit of depression and oppression and I bind and loose any of its effects on my mind and heart. I tear down every stronghold that would try to come against my mind concerning condemnation and guilt. I am the redeemed of the Lord! I am the righteousness of God! I have been forgiven and I forgive myself.

I welcome and receive conviction by the Spirit of God and the continued grace of God to walk in true change. I choose life in my every decision. Even if my heart attempts to condemn me, God does not, and He is greater than my heart and lives in my heart. I'm not moved by accusations from people. I am not moved by the opinions of man. It's settled . . . I will not fall into the condemnation of the devil.

I am abounding in and filled with the fruits of righteousness. I am in right standing with God and right doing—which comes through my Lord and Savior Jesus Christ. I am more than a conqueror, and I gain surpassing victory through Him who loves me.

From this moment forward, I will no longer allow my conscience to accuse me. I have confidence, complete assurance, and boldness before God. I press in this day and every day toward the upward call of God in Christ Jesus. I am quick to obey and quick to repent. Thank You, Father, for taking pleasure in my prosperity—spirit, soul, body, and financially. To the honor and praise of God that His glory may continually be both manifested and recognized in every area of my life. So be it. Amen.

Romans 8:1–3
John 15:3;
2 Corinthians 10:3–5
Philippians 1:11
Romans 8:37
1 Timothy 3:6
1 John 3:21
Psalm 35:27
3 John 2

> When Jesus raised Himself up, He said to her, Woman, where are your accusers? Has no man condemned you? She answered, No one, Lord! And Jesus said, I do not condemn you either. Go on your way and from now on sin no more.
>
> ~ *St. John 8:10–11*

CHAPTER

PROPHETIC WORDS FOR KINGS EDIFICATION

As you read in the author's heart—the introduction you are a King in God's sight just like Jesus. In this chapter you will be encouraged with words of life that will catapult your faith to yet another level that you may continue to fulfill your God-given destiny. Once you are encouraged and stirred up, go and encourage another . . . specifically the non-believer.

> . . . Worship God! For the substance (essence) of the truth revealed by Jesus is the spirit of all prophecy (the vital breath, the inspiration of all inspired preaching and interpretation of the divine will and purpose, including both mine and yours).
>
> ~ *REVELATION 19:10*

"I AM A KING!"

10 Reminders of Your Kingship

1. As born again believers we have been made (previously, already done) kings and priests to God.

   ~ **And has made us kings and priests** (formed us into a kingdom (a royal race) unto God and His Father; to Him be glory and dominion for ever and ever. Amen.

   ~ *Revelation 1:6 NKJV*

2. Jesus is the Lord of lords and the King of kings. Jesus is our King and we are kings.

   ~ And from Jesus Christ the faithful and trustworthy Witness, the Firstborn of the dead (first to be brought back to life) and **the Prince (Ruler) of the kings of the earth.** To Him Who ever loves us and has once (for all) loosed and freed us from our sins by His own blood.

   ~ *Revelation 1:5*

3. The presence and glory of God is seen on all kings in the kingdom of God. His presence promotes life to all those we come into contact with.

~ In light of **a king's countenance is life**, and his favor is as a cloud bringing the spring rain.

~ *PROVERBS 16:15*

4. A king with understanding of their kingship does not commit evil. As the righteousness of God kings go about doing good. Kings submit to God, resist the devil and the devil flees. Kings are ever mindful to keep their foot removed from evil.

~ It is an abomination (to God and men) for kings to commit wickedness, for a throne is established and made secure by righteousness (moral and spiritual rectitude in every area and relation). **Right and just lips are the delight of a king**, and he loves him who speaks what is right.

~ *PROVERBS 16:12, 13*

5. The world will know "the King' as kings (us) walk in their kingship.

~ The king answered Daniel, and said, "Truly your God is the God of gods, **the Lord of kings**, and a revealer of secrets, since you could reveal this secret."

~ *DANIEL 2:47*

6. We are kings in God's kingdom. We have been strategically placed as pieces of the kingdom everywhere. We are to ensure that the kingdom(s) of the dark world become the kingdoms of our God. Only the kingdom of God will last forever.

~ "And in the days of these kings the God of heaven will set up **a kingdom which shall never be destroyed**; and the kingdom shall not be left to other people; it shall break in pieces and consume all these kingdoms, and it shall stand forever."

~ *Daniel 2:44*

7. We can only reign as kings by the power of the Holy Spirit.

~ Counsel is mine, and sound wisdom: I am understanding; I have strength. **By me kings reign, and princes decree justice.**

~ *Proverbs 8:14, 15 KJV*

As kings, we have what we say. We have been made to speak life into existence—just like God did in the beginning.

~ You shall also decide and decree a thing, and it shall be established for you: and the light (of God's favor) shall shine upon your ways.

~ *Job 22:28*

8. Jesus, our Lord, is the King. We are called to be like Him, be as He is and do what He did . . . even greater.

~ I assure you, most solemnly I tell you, if anyone steadfastly believes in Me, he will himself be **able to do the things that I do**: and he will do even greater things than these, because I go to the Father.

~ *John 14:12*

9. We are the image of God. We are just like God.

~ God said, Let Us (Father, Son, and Holy Spirit) make mankind in Our image, after Our likeness, and let them have complete authority over the fish of the sea, the birds of the air, the (tame) beasts, and over all of the earth, and over everything that creeps upon the earth. **So God created man in His own image**, in the image and likeness of God He created him; male and female He created them. And God blessed them and said to them, Be fruitful, multiply, and fill the earth, and subdue it (using all its vast resources in the service of God and man); and have dominion over the fish of the sea, the birds of the air, and over every living creature that moves upon the earth.

~ *Genesis 1:26–28*

10. God said . . . and who can refute what God said?

~ "I said, **You are gods** (since you judge on My behalf as My representatives); indeed, all of you are children of the Most High."

~ *Psalms 82:6*

Revelation 1
Revelation 4
Proverbs 16:12–13

REMINDER OF GOD GIVEN PURPOSE

"The Spirit of the Lord God is upon me; **because** the Lord hath anointed me to preach good tidings unto the meek; he hath sent me to bind up the brokenhearted, to proclaim liberty to the captives, and the opening of the prison to them that are bound; To proclaim the acceptable year of the Lord, and the day of vengeance of our God; to comfort all that mourn; To appoint unto them that mourn in Zion, to give unto them beauty for ashes, the oil of joy for mourning, the garment of praise for the spirit of heaviness; that they might be called trees of righteousness, the planting of the Lord, that He might be glorified."

~ *Isaiah 61:1–3*

"The Spirit of the Lord is upon me, **because** he hath anointed me to preach the gospel to the poor; he hath sent me to heal the brokenhearted, to preach deliverance to the captives, and recovering of sight to the blind, to set at liberty them that are bruised, To preach the acceptable year of the Lord."

~ *Luke 4:18, 19*

"Therefore if any man be in Christ, he is a new creature; old things are passed away; behold, all things are become new. And all things are of God, who hath reconciled us to himself by Jesus Christ, and hath given to us the ministry of reconciliation . . ."

~ *2 Cor. 5:17, 18*

"**Laboring together (as God's fellow workers) with Him** then we beg of you not receive the grace of God in vain (that merciful kindness by which God exerts His holy influence on souls and turns them to Christ, keeping and strengthening them—do not receive it to no **purpose**)."

~ *2 Cor. 6:1 (Amplified)*

WHO I AM

Personal Journal Entry—June 12, 2010
~Transparent, Real, Obedient, & Willing to Share

June 12th—6:20 AM

Praise You, Father, for reminding me this morning of who I really am, and how I should not be caught up nor entangled in fleshly desires, earthly desires, and fleshly emotions.

I am a spirit. I have a soul and I put on this body. My body is last in pleasing. My spirit is first.

I have been sent here. I was placed in my natural mother's womb and put on a body at the time of birth.

I have come to do what my Father in Heaven has sent me to do.

I have come to do the will of my Father who sent me.

Not my will, but His will.

Not my will be done, Father, but Your will be done.

I asked this morning for a fresh anointing to rest upon me to do God's will and fulfill His purpose for sending me.

The body I put on is connected with and part of the earth that was cursed due to disobedience.

So the body I put on wants to live contrary to and in opposition to God's will—the One Who sent me.

Once I received Christ I was filled with and equipped with eternal salvation in the time to come—where I will receive a new body to put on—but in the meanwhile, I have been equipped on the inside and empowered by the Holy Spirit to live inside out.

My natural spirit (who I really am) is now a companion with the Holy Spirit—Who is the Spirit of God. He fellowships and communes with me while helping me to do the will of my Father Who sent me.

The Holy Spirit was sent here. He lives in a body—specifically my body that I put on. He has come to do the will of the Father Who sent Him. He has brought His ministry here. He helps. He comforts. He counsels. He intercedes. He stands by (Isaiah 11:2, 3; 61:1–3).

He brought the very nature of God. He brought the very love, peace, and righteousness of God—making it tangible, real, and experiential.

He brought the wisdom of God. He brought the power of God.

I am a spirit. My spirit is under the lordship of the Holy Spirit since I received Jesus as my Lord and Savior. The Holy Spirit was in—one with—Jesus. Jesus prayed for me (us) to have Him (the Holy Spirit) too while here on the earth.

I am equipped to do the will of my Father Who sent me. I must witness to others the good news of why I've been sent and what is inside the body they see. I must continue to share this gift of the Holy Spirit—that has been sent of God to help all under the lordship of the Christ to do God's will.

Not my will be done, Father, but Your will be done here on earth as it is in Heaven.

~ *TLW*

P.S. It is my Father's will that I use my gift within to reconcile His children back to relationship and divine favor with Him. "**Remind them.**" Yes, Lord!

> "For I have come down from Heaven not to do My own will and purpose but to do the will and purpose of Him Who sent me."
>
> ~ *St. John 6:38–40*

Other scripture references:
Malachi 4:5, 6
Luke 1:17
Isaiah 40:3

STAY WHERE YOU ARE

You Are Being Prepared

"My food is to do the will of Him who sent Me, and to finish His work."

~ *St. John 4:34*

"For I have come down from heaven, not to do My own will, but the will of Him who sent Me."

~ *St. John 6:38*

"Why do you seek Me? Did you not know that I must be about My Father's business?"

~ *Luke 2:49*

Don't move—don't give up—don't quit—keep preparing—keep obeying. You are being prepared for what God placed in your heart. This is the development stage—James 1:2–4. Serving in the kingdom of God at your place of worship is a primary part of your preparation. Do not waver from your confession of faith made at the beginning of your decision to serve in the kingdom—Hebrews 10:23. God is faithful. When it—what God placed in your heart—arrives or shows up—in His timing—you'll be ready as you keep preparing and remaining faithful. He has you in training right where you are—Psalms 37:3–5.

Remain involved with productive things—with things that are moving—kingdom things and plans that you know deep in your heart keep your faith stirred. Your mind will try to cause you to slow down in serving and being involved with what is moving—to toil with what is not moving. What is not moving is anything that is your own agenda and own thoughts about the need to move forward. Yet the bottom line is, it's apparent toil because at the end of the day there's still no fruit and no anointing present or evident. Simply a day of frustration or laziness being spent out of purpose.

Don't let the devil steal your opportunities to keep moving with kingdom business and doing the will of the Father Who has sent you to the earth on assignment. Especially not for mere chump change or temporary fulfillment of old natured desires and ways of making it.

> "Therefore we do not lose heart. Even though our outward man is perishing, yet the inward man is being renewed day by day. For our light affliction, which is but for a moment, is working for us a far more exceeding and eternal weight of glory, while we do not look at the things which are seen, but at the things which are not seen. For the things which are seen are temporary, but the things which are not seen are eternal—everlasting."
>
> *~ 2 Corinthians 4:16–18*

A PROPHET'S PRAYER TO ENCOURAGE HIM/HERSELF

> And I fell at his feet to worship him, but he said to me, "See that you do not do that! I am your fellow servant, and of your brethren who have the testimony of Jesus. Worship God! For the testimony of Jesus is the spirit of prophecy."
>
> ~ *Revelation 19:10*

In the name of Jesus, I am holy just as my God is holy. Therefore, I speak words of life that lead to true change and repentance in the heart of man toward God. The spirit of prophecy operates in and through me. The words of the Lord come not from my own will but by the will of God as I am moved by the Holy Spirit.

I have the spirit of power, love, and of a sound mind. I have been formed in the womb, sanctified and ordained as a prophet to the nations. I will go to all who God will send me. Whatever I am commanded to speak I will speak. I will not be afraid of their faces—God is with me to deliver me.

The words of the Lord have been placed in my mouth. I have been set over nations and over kingdoms—to root out and to pull down, to destroy and to throw down, to build and to plant. The Lord is ready to perform His word. I am covered with the shadow of His hand. I plant the heavens and lay the foundations of the earth with His words.

Whether they hear or refuse, they will know that a prophet has been among them. They are a rebellious house—some even scorpions may bite. I will not be afraid of their words nor moved by their looks. My forehead is harder than flint. I listen and I hear what the Lord will say through me, and I keep my mouth open and eat what He gives me—by refusing to be in rebellion with them.

2 Peter 1:21
2 Timothy 1:7
Jeremiah 1:4–5, 7:10, 12
Isaiah 51:16
Ezekiel 2:5–8, 3:9
Isaiah 50:7
Jeremiah 1:18–19

The Lord God will help me and I will not be disgraced. My face has been set like a flint and I know I will not be ashamed. I am a fortified city, an iron pillar, and a bronze wall against all evil kings, princes, priests, and people that have not been set-up or ordained by God. They may fight against me (spiritually and in the natural) but they will not prevail. The Lord is with me to deliver me. Any and every battle that I may encounter is already won. Victory is already the set outcome. Praise God! So be it. Amen.

PART ONE

HOW A KING STARTS THE DAY FOR VICTORY

CHAPTER

A KING'S MINISTRY TO THE LORD

Ministry to the Lord must come from a pure heart. We are called to worship Him and to worship Him alone. In these next pages you will find heartfelt worship prayers and confessions. I found them most lovely in the early hours of the morning before I said any other prayer or made any other confession. My worship to Him came (and still does come) first. Following worship I would remind myself of my covenant benefits to ensure a fresh day.

> But seek (aim at and strive after) first of all His kingdom and His righteousness (His way of doing and being right), and then all these things taken together will be given you besides.
>
> ~ *Matthew 6:33*

> But without faith it is impossible to please and be satisfactory to Him. For whoever would come near to God must (necessarily) believe that God exists and that He is the rewarder of those who earnestly and diligently seek Him (out).
>
> ~ *Hebrews 11:6*

WORSHIP THE KING OF KINGS AND THE LORD OF LORDS

Holy, holy, holy is the Lord God Almighty, Who was, Who is, and Who is to come.

Worthy are You, O Lord and God, to receive the glory and the honor and dominion! For You created all things and by Your will they were brought into being and were created.

You are worthy to take the scroll, and to open its seals; for You were slain and have redeemed us to God by Your blood—out of every tribe, tongue, people and nation! You have made us kings and priests to our God and we shall reign on the earth.

Worthy is the Lamb that was slain to receive power, and riches, and wisdom, and strength, and honor, and glory, and blessings!

To You, Lord, I worship Who is seated on the throne, and to the Lamb ascribed the blessing and honor and the majesty, the glory and the splendor, and the power forever and ever—through the eternities of the eternities.

The Heavens declare Your glory, O God, and the firmament shows and proclaims Your handiwork.

How great are Your works, O God. A senseless man does not know, nor does a self-confident fool understand, how great and how mighty are the works of my God.

I have breath. I have life. I worship and I praise You, Lord, with my entire being! Thank You . . . So be it. Amen.

Revelation 4:8, 11
Revelation 5:9–10, 12–13
Psalms 150:6

MY SOUL THIRTS FOR MORE OF YOU LORD

O God, You are my God—diligently I seek You. My inner self thirsts for more of You. My flesh longs and is faint for more of You. So I have looked upon You in the sanctuary. I have seen Your power and Your glory—*I have experienced Your presence in the house of the Lord, and I declare that I experience Your presence at home too*. I am flooded with Your very presence, Your very power, and Your very glory!

Your loving-kindness is better than life to me. My lips shall continuously praise You. I bless You while I live—I lift up my hands in Your name. My whole being—*my spirit, my soul and my body*—is satisfied as with marrow and fatness, and with my mouth I praise You with joyful lips.

I remember You and Your goodness upon my bed, and I meditate on You and Your word in the night watches. For You have been my help and You are my help. In the shadow of Your wings I rejoice.

My soul, my whole being, follows hard after You. I cling closely to You, and Your right hand upholds, supports, sustains and defends me. Thank You.

I will not let the mouth of those who speak lies stop me from ministering to You and worshipping You. Those who seek and demand my life to ruin and destroy it shall themselves be destroyed and go into the lower parts of the earth—into the underworld of the dead. They shall be given over to the power of the sword. They shall be a prey for foxes and jackals.

But as a king, I rejoice in You, God! I bind myself by Your authority. I acknowledge Your supremacy, and I devote myself daily to Your glory and Your service alone. In Jesus' name, so be it.

Psalm 63

MY SOUL WAITS FOR YOU GOD AND EXPECTS FROM YOU ONLY

For You, God, alone my soul waits in silence. From You comes my salvation. You are my rock and my salvation, my defense and my fortress; I shall not be greatly moved.

My soul, waits only upon You, God, and silently submits to You—for my hope and my expectation are from You. You alone are my only rock and my salvation. You are my defense and my fortress, I shall not be moved.

With You, God, rests my salvation and my glory. You are my rock of unyielding strength and impenetrable hardness. My refuge is in You!

I trust in, lean on, rely on, and have confidence in You at all times. I pour out my heart before You, God, You are my refuge—You are my fortress and my high tower!

To You, Lord, belongs mercy and loving-kindness, for You render to every man according to his work. I know that You are coming soon and that You are bringing Your rewards with You—to give to every man according to his work.

You refresh and You restore my life—my soul. You and You alone have led me in the path of righteousness *by Your Spirit,* for Your names sake. You have shown me the river whose waters give life—sparkling like crystal—flowing out from the throne of God and of the Lamb.

You are the Alpha and the Omega, the First and the Last—the Before all and the End of all! You are the Root and the Offspring of David and the Bright and Morning Star! Glory!

My soul—my entire being—waits for You, God, and I expect from You alone. I worship You, I pay You divine honors, and I do You Holy service alone. I love You!

Psalm 23:3
Psalm. 62
Revelation 22

KINGS RISE EARLY TO PRAY

"Early in the morning (at dawn), He came back into the temple (court), and the people came to Him in crowds. He sat down and was teaching them."

~ *John 8:2*

O God, You are my God. Early and earnestly I seek You. Your word reminds me that You love those that love You, and those who seek You early will find You—experience Your presence and receive Your wisdom and counsel before daybreak. I'm seeking Your teaching early just like they did in times past . . . I know You are the same yesterday, today, and forevermore.

So Father, I thank You for awakening me morning by morning. I thank You for awakening my ear to hear as a disciple, to hear as one who is being taught. I keep my ear open and I will not turn back or fall alsleep in rebellion or in natural slumber. I receive the early and the latter rain of Your wisdom right now. Praise God!

I seek, ask for, and I receive Your wisdom—for I know You give it liberally and ungrudgingly to whoever asks. I also receive the tongue of a disciple that I will know how to speak a word in season to him who is weary. I receive a mouth and such utterance and wisdom that all my foes and enemies combined will not be able to stand against, refute, or resist it.

I receive the sweet communion of the Holy Spirit early in the morning. I receive His help, comfort, strength, advocacy, standby, counsel and intercession concerning any issues in my heart. My love is set upon the Lord therefore, the Lord has delivered me. The Lord has set me on high because I know the Lord's name. I have a personal knowledge of His mercy, love and kindness. I trust and rely on Him and He will never forsake me—no never. I keep Your commands, my Lord, and this is proof of my love for You. Thank You, Father, for loving me and revealing to me how real You are and for manifesting Yourself directly to me and through me.

I'm determined to seek Your presence daily and early. All will know throughout my day and night season that I have spent time with Jesus! So be it, in Jesus' name I pray.

> "Now when they saw the boldness of Peter and John, and perceived that they were unlearned and ignorant men, they marveled, and they took knowledge of them, that they had been with Jesus."
>
> ~*Acts 4:13 KJV*

Proverbs 8:17
Psalm 91:14
John 14:21
James 1:5
Isaiah 50:4, 5
Luke 21:15

THE BLESSING OF DIVINE PROTECTION

I dwell in the secret place of the Most High. I remain stable and fixed under the shadow of the Almighty—whose power no foe, enemy, or opponent can withstand or defeat! I will say of The Lord, You are my Refuge and my Fortress, You are my God—on You I lean, rely, and confidently (boldly without a doubt) trust!

For You have delivered me from the snare and the evil plots and plans of the fowler (the enemy) and from the deadly pestilence, plague, and deadly diseases. You have covered me with Your pinions, and under your wings I find trust and find refuge. Your truth and Your faithfulness are a shield and a buckler for me.

I will not be afraid of the terror of the night, nor of the arrows (the evil plots and slanders of the wicked) that flies by day. Nor will I be afraid of the pestilence that stalks in darkness, nor of the destruction and sudden death that surprise and lay waste at noonday. A thousand may fall at my side, and ten thousand at my right hand, but it shall not come near me! Only a spectator (viewer and bystander) will I be, as I witness the reward of the wicked. I myself will be inaccessible and untouchable in the secret place of the Most High. Because I have made the Lord my refuge and the Most High my dwelling place, no evil shall befall me. And no plague, or calamity, disaster, or tragedy will come near my tent—near me, near my dwelling place.

The Lord has created over me a cloud by day, a smoke by night and a flaming fire by night. He has covered me, and His glory on me, with a canopy defended by divine love and protection. This canopy provides shade in the daytime from the heat, a place for refuge and a shelter from the storm and the rain. No storm of life will make me fall.

The Lord has given His angels special charge over me to accompany me, to defend me, and to preserve me in all my ways of obedience and service to Him. In their hands, His angels are bearing and lifting me up, and I will not dash my foot against a stone. I will not stumble in sin or fall back into my old ways. As I remain lifted up, I will tread upon the lion and the adder. The young lion and the serpent I will trample under my feet. Every principality, power, ruler of darkness, and spiritual wickedness in high places remain under my feet!

Because I have set my love upon the Lord—because I have purposed in my heart to love Him—as a result, He has delivered me! I know and I understand His name—I have a personal knowledge of His mercy, His love, and His kindness, and I trust and rely on Him—knowing that He will never leave me nor forsake me—no never! This God-kind of love has set me on high above all the nations of the earth.

When I call upon the Lord, He answers me! He is with me in times of trouble, and He delivers always—because I love Him, and I know His

Psalm 91
Isaiah 4

name. He has honored me and has satisfied me with long life. Daily I experience His salvation. Thank You, Lord, for divine protection. Thank You for the blessing upon my life. Amen—So be it.

REBUKING AN EVIL DAY WHILE CONTINUING TO STAND

I am strong in the Lord and in the power of His might! I have on the full armor of God, and I will stand in this evil day. I am mindful that I do not wrestle with flesh and blood, but against principalities, powers, rulers of darkness, and spiritual wickedness in heavenly places, in this earth realm. For my war is not with people. I understand that the days are evil and the earth is getting darker and darker. The word of God cautions that each day will have its own trouble, and I rebuke trouble from entering into my day.

Therefore, I will stand in this evil day. My waist is girded with the truth of God's word. I speak the truth. I live the truth. The Spirit of Truth leads me and guides me into all truth.

I will stand! I have on the breastplate of righteousness. I am in right standing with God. I am the righteousness of God. The glory of God is my rear guard. I will stand! My feet are shod with the preparation of the gospel of peace. I am ever ready to share the good news of the gospel. I preach Christ crucified. I declare that my mouth is the pen of the ready writer.

I will stand! I have on the shield of faith. I am able to put out, to extinguish, and to smother every fiery dart of the wicked one. When the enemy comes in like a flood, the Spirit of the Lord will lift up a standard against him on my behalf. I will stand! I have on the helmet of salvation. I am protected from all evil. I have the mind of Christ, and my memory is blessed.

I will stand! I have the sword of the Spirit (which is the word of God) in my mind, in my heart, and in my mouth. I wax strong on the word of God. I am a student of the word of God. I do not live by bread alone, but by every word that comes from the mouth of my God! My food is to do the will of Him who sent me, and to finish His work. I will say, "It is written!," and evil will bow down and flee from my very presence.

I have on the Lord Jesus Christ. I have on the robe of righteousness. I am fully dressed and clothed with the full armor of God and I will stand in this evil day and when I have done all to stand . . . I will keep on standing!

Finally, I will stand praying always in the Spirit at every opportunity, being watchful and alert, understanding that, as I pray in the Spirit, I will remain built up in my most holy faith (equipped to fight this good fight of faith in which I have already won in Christ)! I have the kingdom of God in me. I am immovable and unshakeable! I am a king, and I will stand in this evil day as a king in my Father's Kingdom here in the earth as it is in heaven! Above all, I am clothed with God's love—the bond of perfection. So be it! In Jesus' name, amen.

Isaiah 52:15, 60:2
Matthew 6:34
John 4:34
Ephesians 6:10–18
1 John 5:4
Jude 20

A KING'S DESIRE FOR THE FATHER'S WILL TO BE DONE

"Jesus said to them, My food (nourishment) is to do the will (pleasure) of Him Who sent Me and to accomplish and completely finish His work."

~ *John 4:34*

Not my will be done my Lord, but Your will be done.

I acknowledge that I, ____________ am able to do nothing of myself (of my own accord). I am able to do 'only' what I see my Father doing—through the examples given in my Lord Jesus and as I hear Your voice. I declare that whatever my Father does I do in the same way. I am able to do nothing successfully from myself (independently, of my own accord) but only as I am taught by God and as I get His orders by the Holy Spirit.

I do not seek or consult my own will. I have no desire to do what is pleasing to myself. I do not seek my own aim or my own purpose, but I only seek the will and the pleasure of my Father Who has sent me. My goal is to assist in finishing His work, just like Jesus did. I am a co-laborer with Christ and I can do all things 'only' through Christ Who strengthens me. I am self-sufficient in Christ's sufficiency.

I hold true to what I have already attained in Christ and I walk and order my life by God's word and God's voice. I am not an enemy of the cross of Christ, the Anointed One. My god is not my stomach, my appetites, my desires nor my will. I do not side with earthly things and earthly agendas. I am a citizen of heaven and from heaven I earnestly and patiently await the coming of our Lord Jesus Christ—the Messiah as Savior.

I thank you Father for Your perfect will done in every area of my life. I thank You for ordering my every step and for making my steps clear. I receive and give thanks to the Holy Spirit for His help as I receive and walk in what You have already done (prearranged and made ready for me to live out). In Jesus name. Amen, so be it.

John 5:19
John 5:30
Philippians 4:13
Isaiah 40:31
Psalm 37:23
Philippians 3:17–20

> "But those who wait on the Lord shall renew their strength; they shall mount up with wings like eagles, they shall run and not be weary, they shall walk and not be faint."
>
> ~ *Isaiah 40:31 NKJV*

RECEIVING ALL THAT HEAVEN HAS FOR THE DAY

John answered, "A man can receive nothing (he can claim nothing, he can take unto himself nothing) except as it has been granted to him from heaven. (A man must be content to receive the gift which is given him from heaven; there is no other source.)"

~ *St. John 3:27*

Father, in the name of Jesus, I receive all that heaven has for me to receive in this day and night season.

I receive heaven's protection.

I receive heaven's provision.

I receive from heaven's economy.

I receive heaven's wisdom—I receive wisdom and revelation from above.

I receive heaven's creativity.

I receive my angelic assistance.

I receive rain and snow from heaven.

I receive seed to sow and bread to eat.

I receive Your thoughts and Your ways.

I receive Your words to speak from heaven.

I receive all that heaven has for me to receive.

I remain in "receive from heaven' mode all the time. So be it. Amen.

John 3:27
Isaiah 55:10

ANXIETY AND WORRY FREE!

Father God,

I seek Your Kingdom first and Your righteousness, and I thank You that all other things are being added to me. Thank You in advance. I do not worry nor do I have any anxiety about anything. In every circumstance and in everything, by prayer and supplication, with thanksgiving I continue to make my requests known to You, God.

I receive Your peace, God, that transcends and surpasses all understanding—keeping guard over my heart and my mind in Christ Jesus. I receive Your promise of rest. I've entered in and I remain in Your rest, God.

I will take no thought nor will I receive a thought on what I will eat, what I will drink, or what I will wear. Those without covenant think on these things. My heavenly Father already knows what I may be in need of. I purpose to think on things that are true—worthy of reverence; things that are lovely and lovable; things that are kind and gracious. If there is any virtue and excellence and anything worthy of praise, I keep my mind set on these things.

I practice what I have learned and received and heard and seen, and I model my way of living on it. And the God of peace is with me. I have strength for all things in Christ Who empowers me. I am ready for anything and equal to anything through Him Who infuses inner strength into me; I am self sufficient in Christ's sufficiency.

And my God will liberally supply, fill to the full, my every need according to His riches in glory in Christ Jesus. To my God and Father be glory forever and ever—through the endless eternities of the eternities. Amen—So be it.

Matthew 6:31–33
Philippians 4:6–9, 13, 19
Hebrews 4:1

EVERY KING PLEADS THE BLOOD OF JESUS

"And they overcame him by the blood of the Lamb, and by the word of their testimony; and they loved not their lives unto the death."

~ *Revelation 12:11*

Father God, I know I am forgiven, cleansed, and protected by the blood of the Lamb which has given me access to the Holy of Holies. Therefore, I enter the throne of grace boldly and through my faith in the blood I take this opportunity to plead the precious blood of Jesus over myself, over my family, over my natural bloodline, and over the entire Church! Where the blood of Jesus is, the destroyer and all evil must pass by.

Therefore, I plead the blood of Jesus over the portals of my mind—I call my thoughts to constantly line up with the thoughts of God. I cast down every vain thought and every wicked imagination that would try to exalt itself against the knowledge of God, and I place my every thought captive to the obedience of Christ. I plead the blood of Jesus over my body—my body will remain consecrated and set apart for God's use only. I plead the blood of Jesus over my will and over my emotions. I also plead the blood of Jesus over every doorpost of all of our homes, over our ministries, over all of our possessions, and over our businesses. I plead the blood of Jesus over our every means of transportation and travel. I plead the blood of Jesus over every building or facility we will enter into, lodge at temporarily or conduct business in (whether to buy or sell). I plead the blood of Jesus over every school and campus ground our children will walk on or attend an event at.

I bind every principality, every power, every ruler of darkness, and every spiritual host of wickedness in heavenly places. I bind every spirit of Belial, every demon spirit, and every evil spirit. I cancel every work and source of witchcraft, sorcery and bewitchment of any occults spoken against us, our families and the Church! I cancel every assignment of Jezebel spirits her daughters and her cohorts. I cancel every assignment of adulteress, seductive, and seductress spirits. I cancel every attempt of queen spirits and goddess spirits—spirits of flattery and manipulation. I cancel all of these demon spirits' assignments that would try to test, tempt, distract, hinder, or remove any of our kingship.

I loose myself and the Church from any and every stronghold and strongman that would attempt to destroy our God-given destinies. We are free and we keep our covenant connection with God through our obedience to the faith. Therefore, we are protected from every attack of sickness and disease. The spirit of infirmity cannot rest and must pass over each and every one of us! I rebuke fear, oppression, depression, doubt, and worry and give these evil spirits no place in any of our lives. Myself and the Church are operating right now by the spirit of power, the spirit of love and the spirit of a sound mind. We are fully clad with God's full armor, and we will successfully stand up against all strategies and deceits of the devil. So be it, in Jesus' name!

> "For the Lord will pass through to slay the Egyptians; and when He sees the blood upon the lintel and the two side posts, the Lord will pass over the door and will not allow the destroyer to come into your houses to slay you."
>
> ~ EXODUS 12:23

Romans 3:25
2 Corinthians 10:5
Ephesians 6:12

PRAYERS FOR KINGS ANYTIME OF DAY OR NIGHT

In this section you will find prayers and confessions for anytime—day or night season—that will minister to you right where you are. As you are led to a prayer by the Holy Spirit, I'm confident it will become personal, and that you will make it your own and expect victory from it.

CHAPTER

THE KING'S CALL TO MINISTER RECONCILIATION

Every born again, spirit filled believer is called to help in restoring man back to the divine grace of God. These prayers will keep this mission in the forefront of your heart, your mind, and in your mouth. These pages of this book touch deep into the heart of God. Those who consider the ministry of reconciliation a lifestyle will truly tap into the secrets and mysteries of God because now you are truly hearing what He desires from His heart—relationship with His creation. Heaven has a vision, and this is the one you should press to fulfill the most.

> Therefore, if any person is (ingrafted) in Christ (the Messiah) he is a new creation (a new creature all together); the old (previous moral and spiritual condition) has passed away. Behold, the fresh and new has come!
>
> ~ *2 Corinthians 5:17*

PRAYER TO RECEIVE THE GIFT OF THE HOLY SPIRIT—POWER

"And he asked them, 'Did you receive the Holy Spirit when you believed (on Jesus as the Christ)?' And they said, 'No, we have not even heard that there is a Holy Spirit.'"

~ *Acts 19:2*

"... how much more shall your heavenly Father give the Holy Spirit to them that ask Him?"

~ *Luke 11:13 KJV*

"For the promise (of the Holy Spirit) is to and for you and your children, and to and for all that are far away, (even) to and for as many as the Lord our God invites and bids to come to Himself."

~ *Acts 2:39*

"But you shall receive power (ability, efficiency, and might) when the Holy Spirit has come upon you, and you shall be My witnesses . . ."

~ *Acts 1:8*

"And whatever you ask for in prayer, having faith and (really) believing . . . , you will receive."

~ *Matthew 21:22*

Heavenly Father,

As Your child, I ask for and I receive the gift of the Holy Spirit by faith!

I receive the baptism and infilling of the Holy Spirit.

I receive the Holy Spirit's power to witness and operate in the fruit of the Spirit.

I receive evidence of speaking in another tongue—the language of my heart where the Holy Spirit lives.

Holy Spirit, take charge of my tongue as I yield my tongue to Your use.

I receive utterance right now! I receive tongues of fire right now!

I am born again and I am spirit-filled with the evidence of speaking in another tongue! In Jesus' name, so be it—Amen.

*Now open your mouth and give it a sound. You are in control. You can start and stop praying in the Spirit at anytime.

> "Therefore, brethren, desire earnestly to prophesy, and do not forbid to speak with tongues."
>
> ~ *1 Corinthians 14:39 NKJV*

Acts 19:2
Acts 1:8
Luke 11:13

RECEIVE ANOINTING TO WITNESS AS MANDATED

Father God, in the precious name of Jesus, I thank you for the opportunity and privilege to be used by you this day to reach out and reap Jesus' harvest! It is a true honor, and I humbly submit myself to the Holy Spirit to have His way and speak through me.

Father, I ask for words and wisdom this day that the enemy can not gainsay nor resist. I ask that You would give me wisdom and understanding in every area that I may lack it. I have the ear of the learned, and I decree and declare that the harvest will not be able to resist the wisdom that will come forth through me by the power of the Holy Spirit.

For I know that it is not by my might, nor by my power that I go out, but it is by the Spirit of the Lord. The Spirit of the Lord is upon me right now (the Spirit of wisdom, knowledge, understanding, divine might, counsel and the fear of the Lord). I am worthy to go out and win souls back into the kingdom of God. I am free from any and all condemnation of the devil. I have no fear. I am anointed to preach and teach the gospel with signs following. God will confirm His word through me, into the hearts that it will be sown into.

As a minister of reconciliation, I decree and declare that I will restore man back to God this day. God has already blessed my good works, and He will be glorified through me. I am being sent this day to heal the broken hearted, to preach deliverance to the captives, to recover sight to the blind, to set at liberty those that are bruised, and to preach the acceptable year of the Lord. Lord, let Your fire be in my hands to heal the sick and cast out devils. Let Your fire be in my tongue to preach and prophesy.

Thank You, Father for signs and wonders—the lame will walk, the blind will see, the diseased will be cleansed, the dead will come to life, the demon possessed will be set free, and the poor will receive their inheritance among the saints in light!

By faith and out of obedience, I go boldly knowing that multitudes this day will receive Jesus into their hearts and confess with their mouths that He is their Lord and Savior! For it is in the majestic, powerful name of Jesus that I will cast out devils and the harvest will speak with new tongues! It is in the name of Jesus that I will lay hands on the sick and they will recover! It is in the name of Jesus . . .

Father, I know that You have already prepared the hearts of the harvest and that I am going where it is ripe and ready! Angels, go forth and bring me into what God has prepared! Go before me and make the crooked places straight. Lord release Your fire and burn up the works of darkness that would try to hinder the harvest from repenting. Let all works of witchcraft and occultism be destroyed from the minds of those I'm going to reap! I come against all anti-Christ spirits, all religious spirits, and all spirits contrary to the Spirit of the Lord.

I decree and declare that, as I set my feet upon the grounds that I have been assigned, I will sanctify the entire area! I declare that the anointing

Isaiah 11:2
Matthew 16:15-20
Luke 4:18

of God will remove every burden and destroy every yoke from the necks of the harvest, and they will freely confess Jesus as their Lord! I am the salt of the earth and a light to nations! Beautiful are the feet of those who share the gospel . . .

A KING MINDFUL OF HEAVEN'S VISION

"Therefore, King Agrippa, I was not disobedient to the heavenly vision, but declared . . ."

~ *Acts 26:13 NKJV*

Father God, I thank You that I am a new creation in Christ; old things are passed away; behold all things have become new! I have been reconciled to God through my faith and my revelation of my Lord Jesus Christ. I receive and I walk in the ministry of reconciliation—I restore man back to God. As I have been committed and made steward over this earthly ministry, I boldly compel man to repent, turn to God, and do works befitting repentance.

I humbly acknowledge my partnership with God and the privilege of serving in the ministry of the Holy Spirit. I am an ambassador for Christ. God pleads through me. He Who knew no sin became sin for me on purpose and for this very reason. I have not received the grace of God in vain. I am the righteousness of God. Praise God! The Spirit of Truth has come and He will guide me into all truth. I will not speak on my own authority, but whatever I hear I will speak and He will tell me things to come.

Therefore, I rise daily and I stand confidently to my feet as a worker together with God. I have not received the grace of God in vain. I am about my Father's business just like Jesus! I am a minister and a witness both of the things which I have seen and of the things which are yet to be revealed. I have been delivered from my former life, and I am sent to open eyes in order to turn many from darkness to light, and from the power of satan to God. Many will receive forgiveness of sins and an inheritance among those who are sanctified by faith in Christ Jesus.

I am obedient to heaven's vision and the ministry of the Holy Spirit through me. Just as Agrippa said to Paul, "You almost persuade me to become a Christian." I declare that I persuade the kings of this world to become Christians in Jesus' name. Every kingdom of this world is becoming the kingdom of my God! So be it. Amen.

> "Arise, shine; for your light has come! And the glory of the Lord is risen upon you. For behold, the darkness shall cover the earth, and deep darkness the people; but the Lord will arise over you, and His glory will be seen upon you. The Gentiles shall come to your light, and kings to the brightness of your rising."
>
> ~ *Isaiah 60:1–3*

2 Corinthians 5:17–21
John 16:8, 13

CONFIDENCE TO MINISTER

Increase of Faith to Minister with Confidence and Boldness

The Spirit of the Lord is on me and operating through me. God has anointed me to preach the gospel to the poor; He has sent me to heal the brokenhearted; to proclaim liberty to the captives and recovery of sight to the blind; to set at liberty those who are oppressed; and to proclaim the acceptable year of the Lord!

The Spirit of wisdom and understanding, the Spirit of counsel and might, the Spirit of knowledge and of the fear of the Lord is on me and operating through me. I have the same anointing as Jesus with the Holy Spirit and with power. I go about doing good and healing all who are oppressed by the devil. God is with me.

The Spirit of truth will lead and guide me into all truth. I will not speak on my own authority, but whatever I hear that I will speak—He will tell me things to come. I receive a mouth, words and wisdom that the enemy cannot gainsay nor resist. I will not be afraid of their faces, for the Lord is with me to deliver me.

Jeremiah. 1:7, 8
Isaiah 11:2
Acts 10:38
Luke 4:18
Luke 21:15
John 14:12
John 16:13

Thank you, Father, for yet another opportunity to serve Your gospel. I humble myself in Your presence, my Lord, and submit under Your mighty hand, that in due time You will exalt me. I receive Your words in the very hour needed. I receive greater works and the confirmation of Your word, not mine. Thanks again for using me to partner in the ministry of the Holy Spirit. I am sure to give You and You alone all the glory. In Jesus' name I seal this confession. Amen. So be it.

DAILY INTERCESSION FOR YOUR FRUIT TO REMAIN

Father God, I pray for my fruit that I have won into the kingdom of God. I decree and I declare that they are remaining strong and steadfast! They hear the voice of God, and the voice of a stranger they will not follow! I pray the anointing, a bloodline, a prayer shield, and a hedge of protection around them. I pray that the fire of God and the angels of the Lord would protect them and cover them. I decree and declare that nothing (no demon spirit, no evil spirit, nor principalities or powers of darkness) will be able to penetrate or perforate the hedges of protection that I have prayed on their behalf. I cancel every demonic assignment, activity, conversation or meeting set up for their day. The anointing upon them will attract the divine—only.

I declare that the Spirit of the Lord is upon them (the Spirit of wisdom, understanding, knowledge, divine counsel, supernatural might and the fear of the Lord) to help them make right decisions this day—decisions that reap life. The anointing of God that is upon them has removed any burdens and destroyed any yokes that may have tried to form in their lives. Father, anoint them to serve You in truth, holiness, and righteousness. I bind and I rebuke the spirit of condemnation from affecting their minds, and trying to hinder spiritual growth in their new life in Christ. Father, continue to cause them to increase in a deeper understanding of Your righteousness that is alive in them, and remind them that they have been set free from their past.

I decree and declare that this day they are filled to the full with the knowledge of God's will in all wisdom and spiritual understanding—that they may walk worthy of the Lord, fully pleasing Him, being fruitful in every good work, and increasing in the knowledge of God! I declare that they are strengthened this day with all might according to God's glorious power, for all patience and longsuffering with joy as they are mindful to give thanks to the Father who has qualified them to be partakers of the inheritance of the saints in the light.

Father send more gospel ambassadors (believers of like precious faith) across their paths to confirm and water the seed that has been sown into their hearts—that they may increase in faith and in the ability to move forward in the Kingdom of the Son of Your love. I pray that Your perfect will be done in their lives—in the earth as it is in Heaven!

Holy Spirit, visit them, teach them, and remain with them—encouraging their hearts and transforming their minds to know the importance of being firmly planted in a sound, bible teaching ministry where they are exposed to the full gospel of Jesus and the ministry of the Holy Spirit. Encourage them to come and worship with me in the house of the Lord! In Jesus' name I pray, and I know I receive. So be it! Amen.

PRAYER OVER SPIRITUAL CHILDREN (DISCIPLES)

> And all your (spiritual) children shall be disciples (taught by the Lord and obedient to His will), and great shall be the peace and undisturbed composure of your children.
>
> ~ *Isaiah 54:13*

I thank God Almighty! I am fruitful and I am multiplying into the lives of others. A nation and a company of nations extend from my witness and spiritual kings come from my body—from the word of God that has been preached from my mouth. I am Zion the city of The Lord. Salvation is in me and is delivered through me. I am a priest of The Lord. Men call me the minister of our God.

I pray a prayer shield, a hedge of protection, a bloodline and the anointing around and over my spiritual children. I declare that no evil will penetrate nor perforate the hedges of protection that I have prayed on their behalf. Angels of the Lord go before each and every one of them and make every crooked place straight. Bring them into all that God has prepared for them. I declare that they choose life in every decision. They submit to God, resist the devil and the devil flees. No weapon formed against them shall prosper.

They are free from fear and they will never be put to shame. God's mercies are new to them daily. Although test of faith will come they will not be moved or shaken. God's love and kindness will not depart from them nor will He ever remove His covenant of peace and completeness from them. I declare that God is directing their every work in truth.

Great is the peace of my spiritual children. They have a personal relationship with God and are taught by God Himself. They hear God's voice and obey. The voice of a stranger they will not follow. They understand spiritual authority and they do not usurp their God-given authority. They operate with willing and obedient hearts. Their lifestyles are blameless as they do all things pleasing in the sight of God and man.

For The Lord is comforting them. He has made their wilderness like Eden, and their desert like the garden of The Lord. I declare that joy and gladness is found in them, thanksgiving and the voice of praise. I declare that all who see them will acknowledge that they are the seed that the Lord has blessed. They go and they make disciples and great is their witness. They too are priest and ministers of The Lord, just like me, just like Jesus. So be it, in Jesus' name.

Genesis 35:11
Isaiah 51:3
Isaiah 54
Isaiah 61:6–8

> Ye have not chosen me, but I have chosen you, and ordained you, that ye should go and bring forth fruit, and that your fruit should remain; that whatever ye shall ask of the Father in My name, He may give it you.
>
> ~*John 15:16 KJV*

WE ALL HAVE A MINISTRY

If you are born again and spirit-filled you have been empowered—just like Jesus—to minister, and to "serve" the gospel to the lost (saved or not).

You have been given the ministry to reconcile man back to God—to restore man back to right relationship and fellowship with God.

"The Spirit of the Lord is upon you. Refresh your ministry. I have blessed your ministry. I have made your name great. Increase. Enlarge. Expand. Your ministry is unique. Use your faith. Be even bolder. I'll do the rest."

Yes, Lord. TLW 6.3.14 : 2P ~ St. Philip, Barbados

2 Corinthians 5:18–21
Isaiah 54
Isaiah 61
Luke 4:18

CHAPTER

THE KING'S CALL TO INTERCESSION

The heart and mind to pray and stand in the gap for someone else is time well spent. This area swiftly moves us from a nature of selfishness to a divine place of selflessness. We can even allow the Holy Spirit to pray through us. When we do this we not only pray for ourselves and our families, but we pray for nations. This is being used by God, and everyone is called to intercede.

> "First of all, then, I admonish and urge that petitions, prayers, intercession, and thanksgiving be offered on behalf of all men. For kings and all that are in authority . . . For such (praying) is good and right, and (it is) pleasing and acceptable to God our Savior Who wishes all men to be saved and (increasingly) to perceive and recognize and discern and know precisely and correctly the (divine) Truth."
>
> ~ *1 Timothy 2:1–4*

CALLING IN LOST SOULS

Father God,

By faith, I release a call out to the lost souls of this world! Repent, and come into the kingdom of God! I call backsliders back to their original place of kingship! I pray forth a hedge of protection and I prophetically stand in the gap for them—that they will not be destroyed. I cancel the enemy's attempt to bring them to their demise. I declare that every one of Jesus' remaining harvest will live and not die to proclaim the works of the Lord!

I put in the sickle, for the harvest is ripe and ready for harvesting! Harvest come! North give up! South keep not back! East and west bring our sons and daughters from a distance! For the time of the harvest is NOW! Lord of the harvest I pray that You will send me forth and other perfect labors out into the harvest, out into the mission fields to preach Christ crucified and share the good news of the gospel. I use my faith knowing that this day thousands will have the opportunity to make Jesus Christ their Lord and their Savior.

Father, I ask that by Your loving kindness, Your tender mercy, and Your heart of compassion (that not one perish)—that You would personally call, invite, and bid them to come to You. As they call upon You, deliver them and save them. I decree and I declare that today is the day of salvation. Multitudes and multitudes that are in the valley of decision I decree and declare they will choose life this day, blessing this day . . . no longer death and no longer the curse.

Lord, remove and discard any veil that would try to hide the Truth from them—the full counsel of Your word. I bind and I loose the spirit of pride and arrogance from them, and I loose the spirit of humility along with the fear of God! I declare that the lost souls will not be able to resist the convicting power of the Holy Spirit nor the wisdom of the Holy Spirit—once released through the perfect laborers who are willing and obedient in sharing this day.

Father, I call every soul and backslider out of darkness into Your most marvelous light . . . out of the hands of satan into Yours. Thank You, for adding souls daily to Your house! As well, I pray for the peace of Jerusalem and I pray for Israel that they all might be saved and come to the knowledge of the truth. Thank You for the opportunity to co-labor with Christ in intercession and in action—doing the true work of the ministry. In Jesus' name I pray. So be it, amen!

Joel 2:32
Joel 3:14
Acts 2:39

PRAYER FOR SPIRITUAL WISDOM AND UNDERSTANDING

Father God, in the name of Jesus, I pray that You grant me and the church the spirit of wisdom and revelation of insight into mysteries and secrets in the deep and intimate knowledge of You.

I pray, Father, that the eyes of our hearts be flooded with light so that we can know and understand the hope to which You have called us, and how rich is Your glorious inheritance in the saints (us—Your set apart ones). I pray that we know and understand what is the immeasurable, unlimited and surpassing greatness of Your power in and for us who believe. I pray that we experience that same power which raised Jesus from the dead and seated Him at Your right hand in heavenly places far above all power and principalities.

I ask, Father, that each of us be filled this day with the full, deep, and clear knowledge of Your will in all spiritual wisdom—in comprehensive insight into Your ways and purposes—and in understanding and discernment of spiritual things—that we may walk, live, and conduct ourselves in a manner worthy of the Lord—fully pleasing to You and desiring to please You in all things—as we bear much fruit in every good work and steadily continue to grow and increase in and by the knowledge of You—having a fuller, deeper, and clearer insight, acquaintance, and recognition of who You are in and through us.

I pray that we be invigorated this day and strengthened with all power according to the might of Your glory—that we may exercise every kind of endurance and patience (perseverance and forbearance) with joy, as we give thanks to You—our Father—Who has qualified and made us fit to share the portion which is the inheritance of the saints (us—God's holy people) in the light.

Father, may our hearts be braced—comforted, cheered, and encouraged—as we are knit together in love . . . that we may come to have all the abounding wealth and blessings of assured conviction of understanding, and that we may be progressively more intimately acquainted with, and may know definitely and accurately and thoroughly, that mystic secret of God, which is Christ the Anointed One.

Grace us with the ability to understand this day more fully that it is in Him (Christ) that lay all the treasures of divine wisdom (comprehensive insight into the ways and purposes of You, Father) and all the riches of spiritual knowledge and enlightment which is also in us who believe! I believe we receive spiritual wisdom and understanding right now in Jesus' name that we may reign as kings and priests and dominate here in the earth as we should. So be it.

Ephesians 1:15–23
Philippians 1:9–11
Colossians 1:9–14

PLEAD THE BLOOD OF JESUS OVER THE CHURCH

> I thank my God at all times for you because of the grace (the favor and spiritual blessing) of God which was bestowed on you in Christ Jesus . . .
>
> ~ *1 Corinthians 1:4*

I thank You, Father, for the Church! I take this opportunity to pray for the Church and I cancel every demon's assignment.

I plead the blood of Jesus over the entire Church. I plead the blood of Jesus over our families, over our homes, over our bloodlines, over our ministries, over our businesses, over our communities, over our cities, over our states, over our regions, and over our nations. I plead the blood of Jesus over all of our possessions and all that we have on every side. I declare the Church blessed. I speak life over the Church, and I cancel every negative word of death spoken.

Satan, in the name of Jesus, I bind you and every one of your servants. I bind every principality, every ruler of darkness, every spiritual host of wickedness, every evil spirit, every demon spirit, every spirit of Belial, every queen spirit, every goddess spirit, every spirit of flattery, every spirit of manipulation, every immoral spirit, every seductive and seductress spirit, and every Sodom and Gomorrah spirit that has been assigned to come against us, test us, tempt us, distract us, or hinder us. I cancel the assignments of these evil spirits against the Church. I declare they will not remove any of our godly kingship. No weapon formed against the Church can prosper. Every liar that speaks against the Church is silenced and proved to be wrong. Greater is He that is in us than he that is in the world! God is for the Church and no one can be against us! I declare new victories for the Body of Christ and I declare we receive by faith.

I come against all prayers of witches and warlocks, as well as all spirits of divination and sorcery that would plot and scheme against the Church with hexes, vexes, chants, and witchcraft soulish prayers. I cancel every prayer of accusation, condemnation, domination, and manipulation that has been released from the mouths of those who are ignorant of God's word and the power of their own words over their fellow brethren—spouses, children, family and friends. I cancel all attacks of mental illnesses, repeated sicknesses, barrenness, family breakdowns, broken marriages, financial insufficiency, accidents, and premature deaths.

The Church is covered in and with the blood of Jesus! We are healed. We have been made whole. We are prospering a spirit, soul, body, financially, and relationally . . . just as our souls are prospering. In Jesus' name I pray, so be it. Amen!

> And He will establish you to the end (keep you steadfast, give you strength, and guarantee your vindication; He will be your warrant against all accusation or indictment so that you will be) guiltless and irreproachable in the day of our Lord Jesus Christ (the Messiah).
>
> ~ 1 Corinthians 1:8

Isaiah 54:17
Ephesians 6:12
Isaiah 13:19
Jeremiah 23:14
3 John 3:2

PRAYER FOR MISSIONS OVERSEAS

Father God, we praise and thank You this day for sending ______________________ and the missions team to minister the Gospel in _____________, and all the surrounding villages and/or communities. Thank You that Your hand is upon them and the Holy Spirit is guiding them each step of the way. Whatever they touch shall prosper. We declare that they are the head, not the tail, above only, and not beneath. We declare that Your favor has gone before them and Your glory will be manifested with them in an excellent way.

Father, in Jesus' name, we believe Your word for the success of this missions trip. We believe and agree together that the Gospel of the Kingdom will cause an indelible impact upon that region. We decree that those who receive it will be totally changed and renewed in the spirit of their minds. We pray that they eagerly receive and believe the Gospel so that they will clearly see themselves reigning as Kings and Priests in the earth. Teach them to hear Your voice and to obey Your word. Protect them from all evil and restore everything that the devil has stolen from them. Cause them to rise up on the inside and give them the desire to rise up out of the bondage of poverty and oppression. Help them to develop bold faith to remove every mountain and bind every devil in their lives. We declare that all the peoples of ______________ will come into the knowledge of Your word and know that they are the redeemed of the Lord. Cause Your Glory to rise upon them as Your Kingdom is established in their lives, their families, and their communities. Cause Your love, joy, and peace to abound toward them and through them. Cause them to know that they can do all things through Christ, the Anointed One, Who strengthens them.

Thank You, Father, for many doors of utterance opened for _______ _____________ and the missions team to proclaim the truth of Jesus Christ. We pray for signs, wonders, and miracles to confirm Your word. We pray for healing from every disease, virus, wound, and abnormality. We pray for creative miracles and the manifestation of all of the gifts of the Spirit. We pray that Your word, mighty deeds, and greater works will go forth in demonstration of the Spirit and of power. We declare that Your word will go forth from every ambassador—unchecked and unhindered by any outside force—and that, as they open their mouths, You will fill them with revelation knowledge.

In the name of Jesus we bind satan, all wicked principalities, powers, rulers of darkness, spiritual hosts of wickedness, and all and any evil princes in the region. In the name of Jesus we bind every worker of evil, used or sent by the evil one. We forbid any evil operation against our missions team, their finances and possessions, travel schedules and transportation vehicles, their health, sleeping accommodations, meetings, meals, and all ministry and leisure activity they will engage in. We cover these areas, our team, the ministries hosting them, every meeting, ministry outreach, and attendee with the blood of Jesus. We apply the blood-line of protection around them, in Jesus' name.

We loose any entanglement of the devil and his workers of evil that may attempt to hinder the success of ______________________ and the missions team. No weapon formed against them can prosper. They are in the right place at the right time with the right information and the right understanding. The Anointing shall abide in every service. The Anointing shall come forth each and every time they minister the word of God. ______________________ gifts to teach will come forth, and his spiritual gifts shall come forth and work effectively and fully each and every time he ministers. Favor is with them and promotion is on them. We thank You for this victorious gift, as You open doors in missions worldwide. Dr. Williams' faithfulness in ministry has made his name great, and nothing but victory will result from this missions trip.

The entire Ministerial team is zealous to perform good works that bring glory to the name of Jesus. As we pray on one accord, we declare that the hosts of hell will be shaken and subdued, and every captive will be set free. Father, we command angels to surround, protect, and fill every city, town, village, road, meeting place, and customs checkpoints. We thank You for the salvation of multitudes of souls, the outpouring of the Holy Spirit, and the Light of the Gospel to overpower and eradicate the darkness, in Jesus' name, AMEN!

BINDING WHISPERERS

> A talebearer reveals secrets, but he who is of a faithful spirit conceals a matter.
>
> ~ *Proverbs 11:13 NKJV*

We bind and cast out all tale bearing spirits. We bind all backbiting, gossip, busybody activity, strife, slander, envy, and jealousy. The mouth of those who speak lies shall be stopped! We bind and cast out all suspicion, distrust, fear, paranoia, accusation, doubt, rejection, hurt, bitterness, unforgiveness, pride, competition, strife, arguing, and fighting. Floods of wickedness may lift up their voices, but the Lord on high is mightier than the noise of many waters. The floods ofthe righteous overthrow and rule!

We rebuke hypocrisy and we bind and cast out spirits of deceit, Pharisees, Scribes, guile, lying, pretense, false love, false worship, false holiness, manipulation, and flattery. We bind mind control. We bind and cast out octopus and squid spirits with tentacles, confusion, mental pressure, mental pain, and migraines. We sever at the root tentacles and every demonic web of confusion, in Jesus name.

We rebuke and drive out 'little leavens', and we bind the spirit of persuasion that would try to hinder people from obeying the truth. This is the house of the faithful!

Holiness adorns this house! This house is blessed! So be it, in Jesus name.

Psalm 63:11 NKJV
Psalm 93:3–5 NKJV
Proverbs 3:33–35 NKJV
Galatians 5:9
1 Timothy 5:13 NKJV

CHAPTER

PERSONAL MINISTRY RELATED (FOR MALE AND FEMALE KINGS)

In this chapter there are prayers and confessions that minister to some personal areas of the soul and the mind of a king with the overall mission of preparation for the soon coming King. These prayers can be prayed by both male and female kings. Our war is not natural but spiritual. Some of these prayers deal with demon spirits that operate in a body to hinder that person from fulfilling their God-given purpose and experiencing the fullness of their kingship here on the earth. Jesus will be returning for a Church that is without wrinkle, spot or blemish. These prayers will assist us in working out our own salvation—from a pure heart.

> For as these qualities are yours and increasingly abound in you, they will keep (you) from being idle or unfruitful unto the (full personal) knowledge of our Lord Jesus Christ (the Messiah, the Anointed One). . . . Thus there will be richly and abundantly provided for you entry into the eternal kingdom of our Lord and Savior Jesus Christ.
>
> ~ *2 Peter 1:8, 11*

EVERY KING HAS A SOUND MIND—NO FEAR!

What is man that You are mindful of him, and the son of [earthborn] man that You care for him?

~ *Psalm 8:4*

I thank You, Father, that You are mindful of me. I thank You for Your thoughts toward me. I thank You that I have been made in Your image and in Your likeness. I receive Your mind and I receive Your thoughts. I have a sound mind. I have the mind of Christ and my memory is blessed. I rebuke any spirit of fear from my mind. I have the spirit of power. I have the spirit of love. I have the spirit of a sound mind.

I am controlled by the desires of the Spirit. My mind is set on—and I seek—those things which gratify the Holy Spirit. The mind of the Holy Spirit is life and peace, both now and forever. I have that same mind, the mind of the Holy Spirit.

I have an understanding mind. I have a discerning mind. I know right from wrong. I know good from evil. I have the mind to choose life in my every decision.

I am redeemed from any demons and curses of crazy, insane, schizophrenic, unsound, batty, demented, sociopath, and irrational thinking. I am blessed and my mind is renewed with the Word of God. I have the mind of Christ. I am free from the mind of my past generations.

I know, I recognize, and I understand in my mind and in my heart that the Lord is God in the heavens above and upon the earth beneath; there is no other. I am always mindful to reverently fear the Lord and to keep all His commandments that it will go well with me and my children forever. God's word is first in my mind and in my heart.

And God's peace, which transcends all understanding is guarding my heart and my mind right now, in and by Christ Jesus. So be it, in Jesus' name.

> And you shall love the Lord your God with all your [mind and] heart and with your entire being and with all your might.
>
> ~ DEUTERONOMY 6:5

Jeremiah 29:11
Deuteronomy 4:39, 5:29, 6:6
Romans 8:5–6
Galatians 3:13, 14
Philippians 4:7

KINGDOM BENEFITS FOR ALL KINGS

"Everything that the Father has is Mine. That is what I meant when I said that He (the Spirit) will take the things that are Mine and will reveal (declare, disclose, transmit) it to you."

~ *St. John 16:15*

Praise the Lord! I thank You, Father God that I am blessed, happy, fortunate, and to be envied because I fear The Lord and I delight greatly in His commandments. My spiritual offspring is mighty on this earth! I am the generation of the upright and I am blessed! I forget not all Your benefits. I thank You and I keep You in remembrance of Your word.

Prosperity, wealth, and riches are in my house and my righteous (in You God) endures forever. Hallelujah! Where ever there is darkness light arises on my behalf, because I am in right standing with You God. All is well with me, I deal generously, I lend and I conduct my affairs with justice (fairness, impartiality, honesty, and integrity).

I will not be moved forever! I am the uncompromisingly righteous and I will be in everlasting remembrance. I will never be forgotten. I will not be afraid of evil tidings (words, reports and communications). My heart is firmly fixed, trusting, leaning on and being confident in The Lord. My heart is established and steady. I will not be afraid as I await the demise of my adversaries and the victory of every test of faith.

I distribute freely to the poor and needy. My uprightness and right standing with God endures forever. My horn is exalted in honor as a result of my obedience.

I am the righteous and it's God's will for me to prosper in every area of my life—spirit, soul, body, relationally and financially. I receive my kingdom benefits and I do my part in keeping God first and above all. I release myself from the trickery of fleeting success and false blessings presented by the kingdom of darkness. I'm in God's marvelous light and my prosperity as a king is promised. The wicked will see it and be angered but, I fret not because the desire of the wicked will perish and come to nothing. I'm equipped to experience the Blessing and I receive the help of the Holy Spirit to see what has already been prepared for me to live the good life! In Jesus' name, amen, so be it.

> "... what does the Lord your God required of you but (reverently) to fear the Lord your God (that is) to walk in all His ways, and to love Him, and to serve the Lord your God with all your (mind and) heart and with your entire being. To keep the commandments of the Lord and His statutes which I command you today for your good? Behold, the heavens and the heaven of heavens belong to the Lord our God the earth also, with all that is in it and on it."
>
> ~ DEUTERONOMY 10:12–14

Psalm 112
Proverbs 10:7
2 Corinthians 9:9

KINGS PUT OFF THE OLD

> Therefore, if any person is (ingrafted) in Christ (the Messiah) he is a new creation (a new creature altogether); the old (previous moral and spiritual condition) has passed away. Behold, the fresh and new has come!
>
> ~ *2 Corinthians 5:17*

I thank You, Father, for my new life in Christ. I choose Christ over carnality! I keep my mind set on things above (not on things beneath). I reject mere mortal thinking, the thoughts of Christ are far better than that! My old man is dead and my new "real" life is hidden with Christ in God. I am born anew, born from above, born by the Spirit. I am alive to righteousness!

Therefore I keep my old members dead. I no longer lie and I have put off all evil—wanting what others have (covetousness, which is idolatry), anger, wrath, blasphemy, and filthy language. I'm determined to keep on the new man who is being renewed daily in knowledge according to the image of Him who created me.

My old man **was** nailed to the cross. My body **was** an instrument of sin. I now declare my body ineffective and inactive to evil. I am no longer a slave to sin. My body is an instrument of righteousness. Sin can no longer rule as king in my mortal body. I no longer yield to its cravings, nor am I subject to its lusts and evil passions.

I keep myself clothed as God's own chosen one. I am purified, holy, and well-beloved by God Himself. I keep on behavior marked by a tender heart, mercy, kindness, gentleness, and patience. I am tireless and long suffering. I have the power to endure whatever comes with a good temper. I will not drawback from the faith I have received by responding to a test of faith with the old nature or old words of death.

I am also determined to choose my companions wisely. I am not deceived nor am I misled. I understand that evil communications, evil companionships, and evil associations can and will corrupt my good manners, morals, and character.

I am the just and I will stay in faith! I am a new man with a new nature. I have fearless confidence. I have no dependence on my flesh. I have no dependence on my intellect. I have no dependence on the worldly wisdom I've received in the past. I am not wise in my own eyes. I embrace and I receive the wisdom, the leading, and the guidance of the Holy Spirit.

Just like Jesus, I have been resurrected to a new life. I receive this new life in Christ. I am not under construction and will never speak these words of defeat again. God is doing a quick work in me as a result of my willingness and obedience to obey His word and walk in His ways. In Jesus' name I pray. So be it.

Romans 6:6, 12
Colossians 3:2–3, 8–10
Hebrews 10:38

A KING DEPRIVING HIS/HER FLESH OF POWER

> For we (Christians) are the true circumcision, who worship God in spirit and by the Spirit of God and exult and glory and pride ourselves in Jesus Christ, and put no confidence or dependence (on what we are) in the flesh and on outward privileges and physical advantages and external appearances . . .
>
> ~ *PHILIPPIANS 3:3*

I thank You, Father, for Your strength and Your power. I am strong in You and in the power of Your might. I put no confidence in my flesh. I actually take this opportunity to use my faith and speak life and truth to my body. I have and I do what I say. I have authority over my body and what I say goes!

I mortify every deed of my flesh. I keep my body under subjection and under the authority of the Spirit of God. I do not fulfill the lust of my flesh. I do not make provision for my flesh. My body is the temple of the Holy Spirit—the very presence of God is in me. Therefore I deprive my flesh of any power that would cause the Holy Spirit to depart from me and cease His ministry through me.

I am consecrated and I am set apart for God's use only. Body, you are no longer used as an instrument of sin! Who I really am is on the inside, and I seek opportunities to feed my spirit-man and not my flesh. I'm mindful of what I put in my ears (what I listen to), in my eyes (what I look at and meditate on), and what I speak from my mouth (any words of death that would draw ungodliness or immorality). I understand that these are the gates (the portals) to my soul. I will not feed my flesh the trash of the devil, nor will I return to the vomit of the past.

I am not ignorant of satan's devices. I can not be moved by flattery. My outer appearance is for the glory of God. When people are drawn to me, it's because of the anointing not because of how I look. My new "real" life is all about Christ the Messiah and His anointing. I receive every opportunity to share Who He is, not who I am.

So, by choice I give my flesh (my body) no power to sin. I am not waiting on God to bring my body to order. I take authority and I call my own body to divine order. I do those things that are pleasing to God and pleasing in His sight. I refuse to be like Esau… I will not sell my soul for a mere morsel. Greater is He that is in me, than he that is in this world. In Jesus' name I pray. So be it.

> Do you not know that your body is the temple (the very sanctuary) of the Holy Spirit Who lives within you, Whom you have received (as a Gift) from God? You are not your own, you were bought with a price (purchased with a preciousness and paid for, made His own). So then, honor God and bring glory to Him in your body.
>
> ~ *1 Corinthians 6:19–20*

Psalm 51:10–12
Ephesian. 6:10
2 Corinthians 2:11
Hebrews 12:16

A KING WITH A PURE HEART

> Search me (thoroughly), O God, and know my heart! Try me and know my thoughts! And see if there is any wicked or hurtful way in me, and lead me in the way everlasting.
>
> ~ *PSALMS 139:23, 24*

Father God, I press to keep my heart pure before You and I thank You for Your grace to do so. I know You search me and know me. You know my inward parts. You understand and know my thoughts. There is not a word in my tongue (still unuttered) that You don't already know about. I declare that I will continue to confess and praise You, for You are fearful and wonderful! How great are Your works! Your eyes saw my unformed substance, and in Your book all the days of my life were written—before they ever took shape. **Search me thoroughly, God,** and know my heart. Try me and know my thoughts! See if there is any wicked or hurtful way in me and lead me in the way everlasting.

I know that You are the Judge and You do not see or judge like mere men according to my outward appearance, nor by any natural accomplishment or stature, but You look directly onto my heart. Thank You, Father for creating in me a clean heart and renewing a steadfast, right spirit within me. Cast me not from Your presence and take not Your Holy Spirit from me. Restore to me the joy of Your salvation and uphold me with a willing spirit. I declare that my heart is **not** deceitful, perverse, corrupt or wicked. The law of the Lord is in my heart and none of my steps will slide. I write Your word, God, upon my heart daily by meditating and studying it—which empowers me not to sin against You.

Thank You, Father, for the understanding that I can choose to tap into, live out of, and draw from Your heart that has **already replaced my old**, cold, hard, stony, and selfish heart—as a born again believer. Today, and every day, I guard my heart with all diligence, understanding that out of it can flow issues of life. I fill my mouth with good things knowing that out of the abundance of my heart my mouth will speak. The only issue in my heart is that it overflows with gratefulness to You, God, for this new life and this new heart of love. I love the Lord my God with all of my heart, my soul, my mind and my entire being.

I am the pure in heart, and I am experiencing God right now and will see the Lord when He comes. Your law is perfect, Lord, transforming me completely. Thank You. I declare that I am cleared from any and all hidden faults. I am blameless, innocent and without guilt. The words of my mouth and the meditation of my heart are acceptable in the sight of God—my Rock and my Redeemer! In Jesus' name I pray. Amen—So be it.

> Blessed (happy, enviably fortunate, and spiritually prosperous—possessing the happiness produced by the experience of God's favor and especially conditioned by the revelation of His grace, regardless of their outward conditions) are the pure in heart, for they shall see God!
>
> ~*Matthew 5:8*

Psalm 19:7–14
Psalm 139
Deuteronomy 6:5
1 Samuel 16:7
Isaiah 51:10–12
Jeremiah 17:9
Matthew 5:8
Psalm 37:31

A KINGS DESIRE TO PLEASE GOD AND NOT MEN

Father God, I pray, and thank You in Jesus' name, that I am filled with the knowledge of Your will in all wisdom and spiritual understanding; that I may walk worthy of You Lord, **fully pleasing You**, being fruitful in every good work and increasing in the knowledge of God; being strengthened with all might, according to Your glorious power, for all patience and longsuffering with joy; giving thanks to You, Father, Who has qualified me to be a partaker of the inheritance of the saints in the light.

I thank You, Lord Jesus for directing my ways and for increase and abundance of love. My heart is established blameless in holiness before You, that I may walk as I ought to walk—**pleasing You, God**. For I know that this is Your will for my life—sanctification that I may remain set apart for God's use—and God's use only.

I trust in You, Lord, and I do good; I dwell in the land and I feed on the Lord's faithfulness. I delight myself also in You, Lord, and I thank You for blessing me with the desires of my heart, I commit my way to You, Lord, I trust in You and my desires come to pass. I rest in You, Lord, and wait patiently for You.

Truly my soul **silently waits for You, God**; from You comes my salvation. You alone are my rock and my salvation; You are my defense; I shall not be greatly moved. My soul waits silently for You, God—You alone. For my expectation is from You. You, Father, only are my rock and my salvation, You are my defense; I shall not be moved. In You, God, are my salvation and my glory; the rock of my strength and my refuge is in You. I trust in You, God, at all times and pour my heart before You.

I am blessed (happy, fortunate, and to be envied) because I earnestly wait for You, Lord. I expect, look and long for more of You. I look and long for more of Your victory, Your favor, Your love, Your peace, Your joy, and **Your matchless, unbroken companionship**—daily! I believe I have received in Jesus' name! Amen.

Colossians 1:9–12 (see amplified)
1 Thessalonians 3:11–13; 4:1–3
Psalm 37:3–5, 7
Psalm 62
Isaiah 30:18 (Amp.)

INCREASING IN THE NATURE OF LOVE 101A

"But woe to you, Pharisees! For you tithe mint and rue and every herb, but disregard and neglect justice and the love of God. These you ought to have done without leaving the others undone."

~ *St. Luke 11:42*

Father God, first of all forgive me for not walking in the nature of Your love in any area of my life—specifically with those who are cruel in their attitude toward me. I repent, knowing that Your word commands that I should bless them and not curse them; that I should pray for them. I refuse to miss any more of my blessings as a result of not cultivating my love walk! **From this moment forward**, in the name of Jesus, I decree and I declare that my love is sincere and it is real! I hate what is evil and I hold fast to what is good. I love others with brotherly or sisterly affection. I give and show honor to others. I never lag in zeal, nor am I slothful. I am fervent and burning with the Spirit, serving the Lord wholeheartedly. I rejoice in hope. I am steadfast and patient in suffering and tribulation, and I am constant in prayer. I heed these things knowing that they could not only hinder my walk in love but also that they can eradicate the spirit of religion.

I contribute to the needs of God's people. I share with the saints. I pursue the practice of hospitality—I am warm, kind, generous and friendly. I bless those who persecute me. I bless them and do not curse them. I rejoice with those who rejoice and I weep with those who weep. I live in harmony with others. I am not haughty—snobbish, high-minded, nor exclusive. I readily adjust myself to people and things and I give myself to humble tasks. I never overestimate myself, nor am I wise in my own eyes.

I endure long and I am patient and kind. I never boil over with jealousy nor am I envious. I am not boastful, nor am I vainglorious—conceited, arrogant, bigheaded or inflated. I am humble. I do not act unbecomingly. For God's love in me does not insist on its own rights or ways, nor is it self-seeking and neither am I! I am not touchy, fretful or resentful. I take no account of the evil done to me and I pay no attention to a suffered wrong. I repay no one for evil. I take thought for what is honest, proper and noble in the sight of everyone, which keeps me above reproach.

I choose to live in peace with everyone—for it is possible because Christ is in me. I never try to avenge or come against the evil that may come against me because God is my Avenger. I get out of the way and leave the way open for God's wrath. For it is written, "Vengeance is Mine, I will repay, says the Lord." I am determined not to be overcome with evil, but to overcome and master evil with good. I bear up under anything and everything that comes my way. I am ever ready to believe the best of every person. My hopes are fadeless under all circumstances and I endure everything without weakening.

The Love of God in me and through me never fails! Therefore I daily pursue, seek and tap into this love—I make it my aim and my great quest! So be it. Amen.

Luke 11:42
Romans 12:9–21
1 Corinthians 13;
1 Peter 2:21

> "For even to this were you called. For Christ also suffered for you, leaving you His personal example, so that you should follow in His footsteps."
>
> ~ *1 Peter 2:21*

INCREASING IN THE NATURE OF LOVE 101B

"He who does not love has not become acquainted with God (does not and never did know Him), for God is love."

~ *1 JOHN 4:8*

I owe no man anything but love. I practice and I cultivate loving others—love is my lifestyle, just like faith. I have fulfilled the law by my obedience to love; therefore I rebuke any spirit of condemnation from coming against me.

I do not commit adultery. I do not kill. I do not steal. I do not covet nor have evil desires for what others have. I do not stray from any of God's commands, understanding that all are summed up in this single one commandment—*that I should love my neighbor as I love myself.* I do no wrong to my neighbor nor do I ever hurt anyone. The love of God that I practice walking in has met every requirement and has fulfilled the law. I understand that this is a crucial hour and how it is high time for all to wake up to this revelation of love and its power.

I know that salvation is nearer than ever before, therefore I drop and fling away the works and the deeds of darkness, and I keep on the (full) armor of light. I live and I conduct myself honorably and becomingly as in the open light of day always. I do not revel, argue, carouse—get drunk. I am not a part of sensuality, quarrelling and jealousy. I remain clothed with the Lord Jesus, and I make no provision for my flesh. I put on God's love daily.

I understand that I will inherit a blessing from God as an heir as I walk in and cultivate "true love." Therefore, I never return evil for evil or an insult for an insult. But on the contrary, I pray blessing, happiness, and protection—truly loving those who are evil, who insult me or open their mouth against me.

I declare that I will continue to enjoy life and see good days! I keep my tongue free from evil and my lips from deceit. I turn completely away from wickedness and shun it, and I do right. I search for peace and harmony with others eagerly. I am mindful not to only seek peaceful relations with God, but with my fellowmen as well.

I remember always that the eyes of the Lord are upon the righteous "kings," and His ears are attentive to my prayers. I am also mindful that His face is against those who do evil—to oppose them, frustrate them and defeat them. No one or word can hurt me because I am a zealous follower of what is good.

I see to it that my conscious is entirely clear so that, if I am falsely accused as an evildoer or threatened abusively and reviled due to my good behavior **of love and life in Christ**, those who accuse may be ashamed. I understand that it is better to suffer unjustly for doing right—knowing it is God's will—than to suffer justly for doing wrong. God is love.

Romans 13:8–14
1 Peter 3:9–12

INCREASING IN THE NATURE OF LOVE 101C

The love of God in me never fails! Praise God! When I was a child, I talked like a child, I thought like a child, I reasoned like a child; now, that I have become a man/woman (a king), I am done away with childish ways, and have put them aside. I am not easily offended, and I walk in the God kind of love.

As a king, I may speak with tongues of men and even angels, but if I choose not to walk in love—I am nothing. Although I may have prophetic powers and understand all the secret truths and mysteries of God, if I choose not to walk in love—I am nothing. As I give to the poor and provide for the needy, but have not the love of God manifesting and showing itself evident in and through my life—I am nothing. I understand that God is Love and all that I desire to do in His kingdom will take His Love through me to prosper me and give Him the glory.

I declare that my love is abounding yet more and more and extending to its fullest development in knowledge and in all keen insight, so that I may surely learn to sense what is vital and approve and prize what is excellent and of real value to God. This day and every day I choose to allow the love of God to abound in me and cause me to be untainted, pure, unerring and blameless, so that my heart may remain pure and that I may approach the day of Christ not stumbling nor causing others to stumble. I am abounding in the fruits of righteousness which comes through the love of my Lord Jesus Christ so that His glory may be both manifested and recognized through my life.

I am a king who keeps and treasures God's word, His precepts, and observes His message in its entirety. Truly, in me the love of and for God has been perfected. By this all know that I am in Him. Any darkness—moral blindness—is clearing away and the true light—the revelation of God in Christ—is shining ever brighter in my life! **I choose life**—light and love. I love my brother and I remain in the Light. By this men know that I am a disciple of Christ because I have love for others.

May the grace (favor and spiritual blessing) of the Lord Jesus Christ and the love God and the presence and fellowship (the sweet communion) of the Holy Spirit be with me and the entire church—always. Amen (so be it).

1 Corinthians 13:1–2, 8–13
Philippians 1:9–10
1 John 2:5-11
2 Corinthians 13:14

> And now abides faith, hope, love, these three; but the greatest of these is love. 1
>
> ~ CORINTHIANS 13:13

NO LONGER A CHILD BUT A SON OF GOD

For all who are led by the Spirit of God are sons of God.

~ *Romans 8:14*

I thank You, Father, for the understanding that I am no longer a child but a son of God, just like Jesus. I am led by the Spirit of God and not by the dictates of my flesh. I walk in and I receive my sonship by faith. I have cried out, "Abba Father!"

I no longer oppose God's will as a son of disobedience. I am free from the (holy) anger of God. I am a son of obedience and I receive my Father's will. I do not seek or consult my own will. I have no desire to do what is pleasing to myself (my own aim, my own purpose), but the will and pleasure of the Father Who sent me. I am able to do nothing of myself, of my own accord. I am able to do what I see My Father doing by and through His word. For whatever the Father (God) does the Son does also. I am a son of God.

I am no longer a child in the kingdom of God but a son tending to my Father's business. I declare that the whole creation continues to see my manifestation as a son of God here on the earth. The Spirit Himself testifies with my spirit. I am an heir of God and a joint heir of Christ. I am going from glory to glory and from faith to faith. I will not draw back from the faith that I have received due to a little suffering or a test of faith.

As a mature son of God, I count it all joy when I encounter trials of any sort. I am assured that the proving of my faith will bring out endurance, steadfastness, and patience. I allow endurance, steadfastness, and patience to do a thorough work in me so that I may be perfectly developed, with no defects, lacking nothing.

I exalt Jesus Christ He is the High Priest! As a son of God, I have been brought into God's glory right here on this earth through Him! I am just like Him. Hallelujah!

Thank You, Father, for Your love and for my adoption as Your own. In Jesus' name I pray. So be it.

Ephesians 1:5
Psalms 82:6
Psalms 22
Romans 8:19
John 5:19 & 30
Colossians 3:6
Hebrews 2:10

> So then, we may no longer be children, tossed (like ships) to and fro between chance gust of teaching and wavering with every changing wind of doctrine, (the prey of) the cunning and cleverness of unscrupulous men (gamblers engaged) in every shifting form of trickery in inventing errors to mislead.
>
> ~ *Ephesians 4:14*

A KING OF NO COMPRISE

The Uncompromising Righteous

Lord, You are on high forever! I praise You for Your goodness, Your love, and Your kindness!

I am the uncompromisingly righteous! I do not compromise, cooperate or negotiate with my old man, old ways, or old thoughts. I am a new man, and have put off the works of my flesh. Therefore, I will triumph in the works of God's hands. My horn God has exalted. I am anointed with fresh oil daily. I have victory over the tricks, schemes and campaigns of the devil. Nothing or no one will stop me from continuing to flourish like a palm tree. I am long-lived, stately, well balanced, upright, useful, and fruitful. I have a sound mind, and I will continue to grow majestic, stable, durable and incorruptible.

I am planted firmly in the house of the Lord and no storm of life will move me. I am growing in God's grace. Hallelujah! Every time I flee and say no to unrighteousness I grow in Him and His righteousness. I am fruitful, and I will still bear fruit in my old age. I am filled with God's fullness. I am full of spiritual and moral vitality, energy, strength, and power. I am rich in the abundance and overflow of trust, love, and contentment.

I am the uncompromisingly righteous. I am a living memorial. I show the world that the Lord is upright and faithful to His promises. God is my rock and there is no unrighteousness in Him. Therefore, there is no unrighteousness in me. I am blessed, fortunate, and spiritually prosperous because I thirst and I hunger for righteousness. I am in right standing with God, and I am completely satisfied and full.

I do my part by seeking God *daily* with my whole heart. I hide His word in my heart, and I let no sin or compromise steal His word from me. I declare that I have the true manifestation of God's fullness in every area of my life. Thank You, God, for the prosperity of my soul. I am becoming (visibly) more like You—inside and out daily. Father God, I love You; Lord Jesus, I love You; Holy Spirit, I love You, and I love my neighbor as I love myself. Holy Spirit, I invite You to have Your way with me. I ask You to perfect those things that concern me. I declare that the **full** purpose of my life will be accomplished! Not part of it, but all of it.

My year has been crowned with God's goodness, and all my paths of righteousness are dripping with His abundance. I am the uncompromisingly righteous, and God will not withhold any good thing from me. I am the uncompromisingly righteous. Surely goodness and mercy are following me all the days of my life. In Jesus' name. So be it.

Psalms 92
Matthew 5:6

A KING'S FRUITFUL GROWTH IN FAITH

May grace and peace be multiplied to me in the knowledge of God and of my Lord Jesus Christ as His divine power has given to me all things that pertain to life and godliness, *through the knowledge of Him Who has called me by glory and virtue,* and He has given me exceedingly great and precious promises, that through these I AM a partaker of the divine nature of God, and I have escaped the corruption that is in this world through lust. Praise God!

Now, Father, in the powerful name of Jesus, because I have been set free and am a partaker of Your divine nature, I give all diligence to add to my faith this day in word and in action! I add to my faith **Virtue** *(excellence, integrity, character, and honesty)!* To virtue, I add to my faith Knowledge—both spiritual and practical! To knowledge, I add to my faith this day **Self Control**—*I control myself. I am not my own; I have been bought with a price, and I therefore submit to God; I mortify the deeds of my flesh; I will not fulfill any lust of my flesh; and I keep my body, mind, will, and emotions under the lordship of the Holy Spirit!*

To self-control, I add to my faith **Perseverance** *(endurance, patience, and steadfastness)!* "Giving up" is not my nature nor am I easily moved or offended. I will stand in this day, and when I have done all to stand, I will keep standing! To perseverance, I add to my faith **Godliness**—*I'm determined to live a holy, godly lifestyle because He that is in me is*

Holy—therefore I am holy! To godliness, I add to my faith **Brotherly Kindness**—*I am kind toward all, especially those in the household of faith! I show no partiality; I am not haughty; and I treat all with respect, honor, and value!*

To brotherly kindness, I add to my faith **LOVE**—*I commit to walk in the God kind of love and I thank You, Father, for preparing hearts to receive Your love through me. I am kind; I'm never envious or jealous; I'm not rude, nor am I puffed up or conceited; I think no evil of myself or others; I am not selfish, nor do I seek my own!* The love of God that is in me always leads me toward the good in others. Above all these things, I am mindful to put on love—which is the bond of perfection. *With love operating, the peace of God rules in my heart. I am THANKFUL as the word of Christ dwells in me richly in all wisdom.*

I decree and declare that these precious promises are mine and I abound in them! I am neither barren nor am I unfruitful in the knowledge of my Lord Jesus Christ. I am not short-sighted or blind, and I have not forgotten that I have been cleansed of my old sins. Therefore, I am even more diligent to make my call and my election sure. My confession and active participation in my new nature will cause me to never stumble or fall. My heavenly reward is an entrance supplied to me abundantly into the everlasting Kingdom of my Lord and Savior Jesus Christ. I will be prepared at His coming. I am born of God and I have overcome the world, and this is my victory that has overcome the world—my faith!

So, this day I add to my faith works (action) which keeps me and my faith alive—alive in Christ! So be it! Amen.

*2 Peter 1:1–11
Colossians 3:5–17*

A KINGS QUEST FOR WISDOM—*ONLY*

Get skillful and godly Wisdom, get understanding (discernment, comprehension, and interpretation); do not forget and do not turn back from the words of my mouth.

~ PROVERBS 4:5

I thank You, Father, for Your great kindness and Your steadfast love! As I walk before You in faithfulness, righteousness, and with an upright heart, I ask for wisdom (only) knowing that You give wisdom liberally and ungrudgingly to all—without finding fault. I receive an understanding mind and a hearing heart that I may judge Your great people correctly. I receive the ability and the grace to discern between good and bad; between the righteous and the wicked; and between those who serve God and those who do not.

I am mindful and I choose not to forsake wisdom. Wisdom keeps me, defends me, and protects me. I love wisdom and wisdom guards me. I understand that skillful, godly Wisdom is the principal thing. I prize wisdom and I exalt wisdom. Wisdom exalts and promotes me. Wisdom brings me honor as I embrace her. I keep firm hold of instruction and I do not let go. Wisdom is my life. I receive from God's Wisdom and I apply God's Wisdom. The years of my life are many. I reject superficial wisdom—wisdom that is earthly, unspiritual, and demonic. I receive undefiled Wisdom that is from above. I receive wisdom that fosters peace, loving-kindness, and gentleness.

I thank You, Father, that because I have asked for wisdom only and not for long life, riches or, for the lives of my enemies—but simply for understanding to recognize what is just and right—that You have blessed me with a wise and discerning mind.

Your word also shares that You are able to do superabundantly, far over, and above all that we dare pray, ask, think or imagine. Therefore, I receive what I have not asked—both riches and honor, so that there shall not be any among the kings of this earth equal to me all of my days. In Jesus' name I pray. So be it. Amen.

Proverbs 4:6–10
Malachi 3:18
Ephesians 3:20
James 1:5
James 3:15, 17

> The Lord by skillful and godly Wisdom has founded the earth; by understanding He has established the heavens.
>
> —*Proverbs 3:19*

THE ANOINTING TO COMPLETE

(It is then) my counsel and my opinion in this matter that I give (you when I say): It is profitable and fitting for you (now to complete the enterprise) which more than a year ago you not only began, but were the first to wish to do anything . . . So now finish doing it, that your (enthusiastic) readiness is desiring it may be equaled by your completion of it according to your ability and means.

~ 2 CORINTHIANS 8:10–11

Father, I thank You for the anointing to complete resting upon me right now to finish what You would have me to complete during this season. I bind all anxiety, worry, doubt, and fear, and I loose great faith upon myself.

I receive Your continued divine order and will to supersede my order and man's order for my days.

I receive Your help, Holy Spirit, to focus on my ministry to You and what You have called me to do—ministry to my spouse, my family, and the church—the way You have ordained and ordered it.

I receive a continual experience of Your peace daily as I fulfill Your divine order and divine purpose in every area of my life.

I thank You, Father, that Your peace is the only confirmation needed to know that I am in the center of Your will—doing exactly what You would have me to do at any given moment.

I understand that it is You, God, by Your Spirit all the while at work in me to will and to do for Your good pleasure, satisfaction, and delight. Thank You. It is not in my strength nor by my power, but it is by the Spirit of the Lord.

Thank You for this covenant of peace. Thank You for helping to order my every step. My mind may plan its way, but it's the voice of The Lord that is directing and guiding my steps! Thank You for the strength to choose Your way, Your order, and Your thoughts.

Proverbs 16:9

My desire is to do the will of Him Who sent me. Not my will, God—not man's will—but Your perfect will be done in every area of my life. I receive a fresh anointing and the grace to "complete" in Jesus' name. So be it! . . . I love You.

INCREASE IN THE ABILITY TO DISCERN SPIRITS

> Beloved, do not put faith in every spirit, but prove (test) the spirits to discover whether they proceed from God; for many false prophets have gone forth into the world.
>
> ~ 1 JOHN 4:1

Father, I thank You for the ability to discern between the righteous and the wicked, between him who serves You and him who does not.

I know, I perceive, and I recognize the Spirit of God—by every spirit that acknowledges the truth that Jesus Christ actually became man and has come in the flesh (this one proceeds from God). I know, I perceive, and I recognize the spirit of the antichrist—by every spirit that "does not" acknowledge the truth that Jesus Christ actually became man and has come in the flesh (this one "does not" proceed from God). By this I know and discern the Spirit of Truth and the spirit of error.

I understand that in the last days there will come perilous times and that some will hold a form of true religion (ministers of darkness) but deny and reject and are strangers to the power of it. I am admonished and warned to avoid such people and to turn away from them—lovers of self, self-centered, lovers of money, greedy, proud, arrogant, contemptuous boasters, abusive, disobedient to parents, ungrateful, unholy, those without human affection, callous, slanderers, false accusers, troublemakers, those loose in morals and conduct, uncontrolled, haters of good, self-conceited, and lovers of sensual pleasures rather than lovers of God.

I am mindful that he who does not love has not become acquainted with God. I understand that God is love.

I also take heed to myself. I am the just and I live by faith. I'm determined not to draw back from the faith that I have received. I am of God. I belong to God. I have already defeated and overcome the agents of the antichrist. Greater and mightier is He Who lives in me than he who is in the world. In Jesus' name I pray. So be it.

Malachi 3:18
Hebrew10:38
2 Timothy 3:1–5
1 John 4:2–4

> But the Holy Spirit distinctly and expressly declares that in latter times some will turn away from the faith, giving attention to deluding and seducing spirits and doctrines that demons teach, through the hypocrisy and pretensions of liars whose consciences are seared (cauterized).
>
> *~ 1 Timothy 4:1–2*

OVERCOME ARROGANCE AND WALK IN HUMILITY

Pride goes before destruction, and a haughty spirit before a fall. Better it is to be of a humble spirit with the meek and poor than to divide the spoil with the proud.

~ *Proverbs 16:18–19*

I thank God for the grace to humble myself. I know God resists the proud and gives grace to the humble. Therefore, I humble myself under the mighty hand of God and in the sight of the Lord. He lifts me up. I humble myself as a child before God and this attitude (with action) keeps me great in the kingdom of heaven.

I will not allow the enemy to use pride and arrogance as a weapon against me, against me fulfilling my divine destiny. I rebuke the adversary. I rebuke the roaring lion that walks about seeking who he may devour. I resist him by faith, and I cast every care upon the Lord. I know He cares for me. My humility keeps me sober and sound in my mind.

I am mindful of the seven things the Lord hates and a proud look is one. I bind all pride from my life. I rebuke every proud look from my eyes. I do not overestimate myself and underestimate others. I am not wise in my own conceits. I will not allow pride to bring me low. My humble spirit is upheld by honor.

Therefore I submit myself to God. I resist the devil, and he has fled from me. I draw continuously to God, and He draws nigh to me. My hands are cleansed from pride and arrogance. My heart is contrite and pure. My mind is no longer double minded. The Lord forgets not the humble. I choose to walk in humility and the fear of the Lord. In Jesus' name, so be it. Amen.

Proverbs 6:16–17
Psalms 10:12
Proverbs 29:23
Romans 12:16
Matthew 18:4
Matthew 23:12
James 4:6–8, 10

> For thus saith the high and lofty One that inhabiteth eternity, whose name is Holy; I dwell in the high and holy place, with him also that is of a contrite and humble spirit, to revive the spirit of the humble, and to revive the heart of the contrite ones.
>
> ~ *Isaiah 57:15 KJV*

RECEIVE KINGDOM MYSTERIES REVEALED

> But as it is written, "Eye hath not seen, nor ear heard, neither have entered into the heart of man, the things which God hath prepared for them that love him."
>
> ~ *1 Corinthians 2:9 KJV*

Father, in the powerful name of Jesus, I love You and I receive my eyes open, and my ears open, and my heart open continuously to hear, to see, and to receive the entrance of all that you have already made and prepared for me as a king throughout my reign here in the earth realm. I'm reminded in Proverbs 3:32, that Your confidential communion and secret counsel are with the uncompromisingly righteous. Praise God, that's me!

By faith I receive Your mysteries revealed and unveiled by and through Your Spirit to my spirit. I understand that it's the Holy Spirit that searches all things—yes, the bottomless, profound things of God. I have not received the spirit that belongs to this world, but the Holy Spirit Who is from You, God, that I may know, experience, comprehend, and appreciate the gifts and divine favor that has been so freely given to me by You.

It is Your glory to reveal a thing to your sons, and it is my honor to seek them out—diligently. I give You the glory as I seek out what You have already done by receiving it in my heart and seeking Your word and listening to Your voice. It has been given to me to know the mystery of the kingdom of God, and not to the sons of men who are without the Holy Spirit. Thank You, Father, for such an awesome privilege.

I'm reminded, Father, that Your word shares that the secret things belong to the Lord our God, but the things which are revealed belong to us and to our children forever that we may do all of the words of this law. Also, Your word shares that You will do nothing without first revealing Your secrets to Your servants the prophets. Whether, I hold the office of a prophet or not, I know I speak life and I prophesy life to others as a born again believer is commanded. Therefore, I receive Your secrets revealed and clearly made known concerning my destiny.

Spirit of Truth, as I pray in the Spirit, I receive You speaking forth God's mysteries through me. Continue to declare what is right to me, Father. I hear Your voice clearly, and the voice of a stranger I will not follow. I hear what You say and I do what I hear, and I am daily walking in Your counsel and experiencing what could have never been revealed to my senses or my flesh. I receive kingdom mysteries revealed. I know You are not withholding any good thing from me, and I thank You in advance. So be it. Amen.

Deuteronomy 29:29
Proverb 25:2
Isaiah 45:19
Amos 3:7
Mark 4:11
1 Corinthians 14:2
2 Corinthians 2:9–12

> The secret things belong unto the Lord our God, but the things which are revealed belong to us and to our children forever, that we may do all the words of this law.
>
> ~ *Deuteronomy 29:29*

VICTORY OVER KINGSHIP REMOVERS

> Give not your strength to (loose) women, nor your ways to those who and that which ruin and destroy kings.
>
> ~ PROVERBS 31:3

I am strong in the Lord and in the power of His might. I mortify every deed of my flesh, and I do not fulfill the lust of my flesh. I recognize and I acknowledge the great call of God on my life. I will not give my strength to loose women, nor will I give my ways to those who ruin and destroy kings. I have victory over every kingship remover that the enemy would try to send across my path. I am a king in the kingdom of God. I am not wise in my own eyes, and I am not ignorant of satan's devices to get me off course.

King Solomon may have been captured by strange women and his kingship removed, but I declare that I will not miss the mark! I do not lust after beauty—understanding that charm and grace are deceptive and beauty is vain—*it does not last.* Neither am I captured by the eyelids of a harlot. I break the power of spells by witches and warlocks that transmit through their eyes and/or by their touch. My eye is single, therefore my whole body is full of light. I remove my foot from evil and I walk free from "second looks". I am mindful that it is on account of a harlot that a man is brought to a piece of bread and that the assignment of the adulteress is to stalk and snare the precious life of a man as if with a hook.

I declare that discretion watches over me and understanding keeps me, to deliver me from all alien women—those who do not fear God and worship Him—those who flatter with their words and forget her covenant with God. I have knowledge that her house sinks down to death, and her paths to the spirits of the dead. No one who goes to her returns again. I walk in the way of a good man and I keep to the path of the consistently righteous. I dwell in the land of men of integrity, (blameless and complete in God sight) . . . understanding that the wicked will be cut off from experiencing the blessing of God.

I choose to live right and heed the commands of God. I walk in the wisdom of God concerning my kingship, understanding that I am not wrestling with flesh and blood *only,* but with principalities, rulers of darkness and spiritual wickedness in heavenly places. Therefore, I take authority and I cancel every assignment of Jezebel, (adulteress and seductive spirits)! I cancel every assignment of queen spirits and goddess spirits! I cancel every assignment of familiar spirits—spirits of flattery and manipulation that would try to test, tempt, distract, or hinder me from fulfilling my God-given destiny daily, and remaining faithful to God and my relationship with Him by His Spirit. No weapon formed against me will prosper.

I flee the very thought of committing adultery against God understanding that whoever does so destroys his own life. Wounds and disgrace are his rewards. I walk in moral principle and prudence. I have good sense. I lay the commands of God in my heart. I live them and do them. I treat skillful and godly Wisdom as my sister, and I regard understanding and insight as my intimate friend. This keeps me from the ambush of the loose woman and from the adventures of one who flatters with her tongue and makes smooth the words of her mouth.

I am mindful of the twilight and the evening—the season of the harlot and divine time of the harlot. I am not captured by the underlying cunningness of the devil through billboards, television, and magazines that display these demon spirits in human form. I am mindful of what I feed my flesh, (eyes, ears and mind), with. I tear down any former strongholds and root out any demonic visuals, images, and pictures that have not been planted by my Father in Heaven. I meditate on God's word—not images, illusions, mirages or fantasies.

I declare that my heart is perfect, complete and whole, towards God and I cling to His love. I do not seek love from other gods. I do my part by removing my foot from evil, submitting to God, and resisting the devil. I choose life, understanding that no one can make me sin or miss the mark. No demon or devil has power over me. It's a choice and I choose life, as I have been commanded in Deuteronomy 30:19. So be it. Amen.

> Did not Solomon king of Israel act treacherously against God and miss the mark on account of such women? Among many nations there was no king like him. He was loved by his God, and God made him king over all Israel; yet strange women even caused him to sin (when he was old he turned treacherously away from the Lord to other gods, and God rent his kingdom from him.)
>
> ~ *Nehemiah 13:26*

1 Kings 11:1–11
Nehemiah 13:26
Proverbs 2:16–20
Proverbs 6:25, 26, 32, 33
Proverbs 7
Proverbs 29:3
Proverbs 31:3
Matthew 15:13

HEALING FOR HURTING WOMEN—ABUSED BY WORDS

I take authority right now in the name of Jesus, and I declare healing and restoration for my soul, mind, and body. I declare that I am made whole—nothing emotionally missing and nothing emotionally needed.

I cancel the power of flaming darts and missiles that have come against me in the form of words. Every evil word and/or plant in me—that the Heavenly Father has not planted—I root out right now by speaking and declaring this prayer.

I curse all bitterness at the root that would try to eat away at my heart and my reproductive organs. I rebuke sickness from prospering in any shape, form, or fashion in my body. I pull down strongholds of defeat, failure, and blame against myself.

I pray for the comforting power of The Holy Spirit and I receive. Holy Spirit, perfect those things that concern me.

I declare that the peace of God is guarding my heart and my mind in and by Christ Jesus—right now.

I forgive those who have trespassed against me. I forgive and I forget. Holy Spirit, help me to do this and to cultivate a forgiving lifestyle daily as I move forward boldly fulfilling my God given purpose. I declare that no distraction of unforgiveness will slow me down from my partnership with You—Holy Spirit.

I know who I am and Whose I am! I am a daughter (a king) of the most High God, and He fights my every battle. I have the victory! He will not ever—no never- leave me nor forsake me. He is my rock and my unyielding strength. He is my strong tower and my stronghold. All other stronghold's that are not of God are broken now!

I have newness in Christ. I declare that old things have passed away and I receive the new. The past has no power over me, and will not capture me with depression and/or oppression. I am free. I receive the garment of praise and the oil of joy. Thank You, Father!

I plead the blood of Jesus over myself and over any other woman covered by this prayer. I am mindful to daily put on the full armor of God, so that I will be strong in the Lord—always protected in these evil days . . . against a fool's mouth.

Behold, I remind myself that I have been given the authority to trample over all the power of the enemy, and nothing will by any means hurt me. I walk in my God given authority and I receive the victory of a sound mind.

My spirit is not broken nor is my heart. I receive refreshing from God. I am healed of hurt, made whole, and the peace of God is being still right now in and through me. So be it. Amen.

Philippians 3:13 & 4:7
Jeremiah 8:11
Luke 10:19
Matthew 15:13
Matthew 6:14
2 Corinthians 5:17
2 Corinthians 10:4
Ephesians 6:10–18
Proverbs 18:14

TAMING A TONGUE ON FIRE

Father God, I receive a mouth—words and wisdom that the enemy cannot gainsay nor resist. I let my "yes" be "yes" and my "no" be "no," understanding that anything more than that is of the evil one.

I understand that the tongue is a fire and can be used as a world of wickedness—contaminating and depraving my whole body and setting on fire the cycle of the carnal nature (my flesh)—being itself ignited by hell.

In the name of Jesus, I bind the spirit of clamor that would cause me to talk too much and run my mouth loosely. I am not a foolish woman who is talkative, clamorous and boisterous. I keep my tongue from evil and my lips from speaking deceit. I keep false and dishonest speech away from me, and willful and contrary talk I keep far from me.

I tame, discipline, and cultivate my tongue by choosing to do so. I understand that my tongue can be restless (undisciplined and irreconcilable) evil, full of deadly poison. With the tongue we bless the Lord and Father, and with it we curse men who were made in God's likeness. This is not so in my life nor in my mouth! I declare that out of my mouth proceed blessing and not cursing.

I choose to open my mouth in skillful and godly wisdom, and on my tongue is the law of kindness—giving counsel and instruction. I look well to how things go in my household, and the bread of idleness (gossip, discontent, murmuring, complaining, and self-pity) I will not eat.

As a female king in the kingdom of God—here on this earth—I decree and I declare that I am free from talking too much and using idle words. Sin is lacking in my life and has no place in me because my words are not with multiplication. I choose tongues of fire by the Holy Spirit that reap life in me and in those who will hear, **instead of** tongues of fire from the pit of hell that will reap death in me and those who will hear.

Matthew 5:37
James 3
Proverbs 9:13
Proverbs 10:19
Psalms 34:13, 14
Proverbs 31:26–27

I depart from evil and do good. I seek peace and I pursue it—specifically with the choice of my words. So be it. Amen.

A WOMAN CONFRONTING THEIR MIND

I **tear down** all strongholds of the devil that would try to come against my mind. I cast down all arguments and vain, wicked imaginations (every high thing that would try to exalt itself against the knowledge of God) from penetrating my mind and heart. I bring every thought captive to the obedience of Christ.

I come against all earthly, sensual and demonic wisdom. I come against misunderstanding, sensible thoughts, carnal and foolish thinking. I come against being wise in my own natural eyes.

I bind and I loose all ungodly thoughts. I bind and I loose the spirit of fear, the spirit of unbelief, the spirit of doubt, the spirit of confusion, the spirit of worry and any spirit that would try to debate the word of God from manifesting fully in my heart. I decree and declare that I have the mind of Christ. I hold His very thoughts, feelings, and purposes in my heart.

I receive a sound, balanced, stable, sober, temperate mind right now, in the name of Jesus! I receive the mind of Christ. I decree and declare that all my thoughts are now under the authority of and made subject to, the Lordship of Christ. I hold the very thoughts, feelings and purposes of Christ in my heart.

I call forth a shift from my mind region. Any wisdom and revelation that I have received as a download from the Holy Spirit that may be caught between my soul and spirit, I decree its release into my heart right now!

I decree and declare INSTANT understanding and INSTANT receiving of God's word by my spirit-man from this moment forward! Information that was in my mind has now become revelation, wisdom and full understanding in my heart! The word of God will not—and can not—be stolen from me ever again! In Jesus' name I pray. Amen.

> "The more time you spend with the Holy Spirit, praying in the Spirit, hearing from the Spirit, and being more sensitive to the Spirit of God you will become more equipped in your mind/soul not to resist the Spirit of God and His wisdom—which will give you full understanding of God's word—leading to fullness in every area of your life." "Also . . . be mindful to repent if you have made a mistake. Those that remain bound to their sins don't feel worthy in His presence."
>
> ~ **TLW**

2 Corinthians 10:4–6

A WOMAN FREE FROM THE WORLD'S SYSTEM

I decree and I declare that, as a daughter of the Most High God, and a king in the kingdom of God, I am free from this world's system!

I am free from welfare, food stamps, social security, W.I.C., and all other systems set-up to try and keep me dependent on man and not on God as my only Source!

I loose myself from any soulish and generational dependency upon these resources, in Jesus' name! I am the redeemed of the Lord, and I have been set free from the curse of the law (this world system)!

God is my Source! Jehovah-Jireh is my Provider! El Shaddai has met my every need! I declare that money is coming right now to me, and every other righteous woman who has been caught in this deception—from here to the ends of the earth.

I decree and declare that I and my sisters in Christ have a revelation and insight of what God's purpose is for our lives, and we pray for God's continued guidance and wisdom.

The door that God has opened for us to walk in for employment and entrepreneurship—we walk in without fear of losing the stronghold of the illusive benefits of the world's system. Whatever check we give up—out of obedience to God's voice to walk by faith and not by sight—God is going to replace it sevenfold, and provide for us greater than we could have ever imagined.

From this moment forward, I am determined not to worry or be anxious about what to eat, what to drink, or what to wear for my household. I declare that we diligently seek the kingdom of God! Every bill is paid. Every need is met, and we believe and know that all other things will be added to us, in Jesus' name! So be it. Amen.

Matthew 6:31–34
Galatians 3:13, 14
Ephesians 1:17
Philippians 4:13
James 1:5

I AM A VIRTUOUS WOMAN!

Father, I thank You that I am a virtuous woman! I am far more precious than jewels and my value is far above rubies or pearls. The heart of my husband trusts in me confidently and relies on and believes in me securely. I declare that he has no lack of honest gain and no need of dishonest spoil. I will comfort, encourage, and do him only good as long as there is life in me.

I seek out ways to work willingly with my hands. I am like the merchant ships loaded with harvest, products and goods. I bring my household food from afar. I rise while it is yet night and I get spiritual food for my household and assign my maids their tasks. I consider a new field (I own properties) before I buy or accept it—expanding prudently and not courting neglect of my present duties by assuming other duties. With the savings of my time, strength, and finances I plant fruitful vines in my vineyard.

I gird myself with strength—spiritual, mental, and physical fitness for my God-given task—and I make my arms strong and firm. I taste and see the evidence and gain from my work—with and for God—and it is good. My lamp goes not out but burns on continually through any troubles—warring away fear, doubt and distrust. I lay my hands to the spindle and my hands hold the distaff. Yes, my hands are open to the poor, and I reach out my filled hands to the needy. I fear not, my entire household is doubly clothed with the blood of Jesus.

I am creative in how I cloth my body. My clothing is fine, pure, and linen—just as it should be for a king. My husband is known in the city's gates—when he sits among the elders of the land. I make fine products—whatever their genre may be—and I lead others to buy them. I deliver them to the distributors or merchandisers. Strength and dignity are my clothing, and my position is strong and secure. I rejoice over the future—free from worry and anxieties—knowing that I and my family are ready for it! I open my mouth in skillful and godly Wisdom, and on my tongue is the law of kindness—giving counsel and instruction. I look well to how things go in my household, and the bread of idleness (gossip, discontent, murmuring, complaining, and self-pity) I will not eat!

My children—both spiritual and natural—rise up and call me blessed (happy, fortunate and to be envied). My husband boasts and praises me saying, "Many daughters have done virtuously, nobly, and well (with the strength of character that is steadfast in goodness), but you excel them all." I understand that charm and grace are deceptive, and that beauty is vain (because it does not last). I am a woman who reverently and worshipfully fears the Lord, and I shall continue to be praised. I receive the fruit of my hands. I let the evidence of my works praise me in the land, as my God receives the glory through me—in my city, state, region, and nation and throughout the entire world. Amen, (so be it).

Proverbs 31:10–31

GOD'S MEDICINE FOR LONG LIFE

> A happy heart is good medicine and a cheerful mind works healing, but a broken spirit dries up the bones.
>
> ~ *Proverbs 17:22*

As a born again, son of God I forget not the law or teaching, but I let my heart keep God's commandments; for length of days and years of a life (worth living) and tranquility (inward and outward and continuing through old age till death), is added to me. God's word is health to my nerves and sinews (my ligaments and muscles), and marrow (my heart and my soul) and moistening (moisture) to my bones.

I trust in the Lord. I am healed and protected by my covenant relationship with Him. With long life will He satisfy me and show me His salvation. I live completely satisfied in Him.

God gives power to the faint and weary and to him who has no might. I declare that God is increasing my strength right now (making it to abound). I am not tired, nor am I weary. I am full of spiritual vitality, and I am rich in the abundance of trust, love, and contentment.

The Lord has taken away from me all sickness (spiritual darkness and death). The curse has been driven away from me with the blood of Jesus! I am immune (not subject) to physical infirmity, disease, addiction, fear, weakness, and every kind of mental and emotional torment.

My Lord Jesus has borne every grief, sickness, weakness and distress, and has carried every sorrow and pain far from me. Thank You, Lord! With the stripes that wounded Jesus, I am registered in heaven and in this earth as healed and whole. I take my healing, and I receive my healing in Jesus' name!

I have long life and good life still ahead of me. I am a "living" memorial to show that the Lord is upright and faithful to His promises. He is my Rock, and there is no unrighteousness in Him. He is not a liar, nor does He endorse evil reports against my body. God is true and every unrighteous man a liar. I receive the promise of eternal life. I am quick to obey, quick to love, and quick to repent. So be it. Amen.

Proverbs 3:1–2, 8
Psalm 91:16
Psalms 92:15
Isaiah 40:29
Deuteronomy 7:15
Isaiah 53:4–5
Psalm 103:4–5
1 John 2:25

LIVING THE LIFESTYLE OF THE HEALED

Search me (thoroughly), O God, and know my heart! Try me and know my thoughts! And see if there is any wicked or hurtful way in me, and lead me in the way everlasting.

~ *PSALMS 139:23–24*

By faith, I live the lifestyle of the healed! I am the humble and I am glad. I seek God and my heart lives. I seek first God's kingdom and His righteousness. I receive all other things added to me—specifically divine health. I feed on God's word. God satisfies my mouth with good things, and my youth is renewed like the eagles. Thank You, Father!

I am disease free and I have maximum health. My body is the temple of the Holy Spirit. I exercise regularly and my heart is pure. I treat people right. I do not overestimate myself and underestimate others. I operate and I flow by the fruit of the Holy Spirit. I seek knowledge and understanding concerning optimum health. I apply God's wisdom to what I hear and learn that relates to me personally.

I also exercise my God-given dominion and authority over my body. I keep my body under authority and submission. I do not fulfill any lust or cravings of my flesh. I choose to eat living foods instead of processed, dead foods. I am mindful to target my intake of specific antioxidants, vitamins, and minerals. I eat healthy fats, whole grains, fruits, and vegetables—all in the appropriate serving size. I do not indulge or overeat in these areas.

I am victorious over the curse of pre-mature death with the knowledge of God's word and the action of my faith! I will live and not die to proclaim the works of my God! Thank You, Father, for Your promise of a prosperous soul. I receive continued prosperity—spirit, soul, and body. I live the lifestyle of the healed and I am blessed in every area of my life! In Jesus' name I pray. Amen, so be it.

> I have strength for all things in Christ Who empowers me (I am ready for anything and equal to anything through Him Who infuses inner strength into me; I am self-sufficient in Christ's sufficiency).
>
> ~ PHILIPPIANS 4:13

Psalms 69:32
Psalms 103:5
1 Timothy 4:7–8
3 John 2

THE DEVIL'S CAMPAIGN AGAINST MARRIAGES *CANCELLED!*

I decree and declare that my husband/wife, _______________, and I, _________________, are free from the lust of the eyes, the lust of the flesh and the pride of life. We are free from eyes of adultery and free from a heart of idolatry. Deliverance comes to us in the night season. Even while we sleep we are being divinely delivered from any thoughts, visuals, campaigns, and strongholds that are not godly. I loose godly strongholds over every area of our lives. I decree and declare that our thoughts, our actions and our attitudes are dictated by our spirit, and not by our flesh. We mortify the deeds of our flesh daily, and do not fulfill the lust of it, nor make provision for it.

We are kings in God's kingdom and priests unto the Lord, and we act accordingly. I bind and I rebuke the attempts of any Jezebel spirits that would try to remove our kingship. The campaigns of the devil cannot and will not capture our eyes of flesh, because our spiritual eyes over rule our vision. We are not moved by flattery. We instantly recognize the attempts of flattery, and we resist. I remind spirits of lust and perversion that they have no authority or power over our lives. We have dominion over them! Familiar spirits are rejected because of the anointing that rests upon us. We are not ignorant of satan's devices or campaigns to bring division, strife or confusion, and he is well aware of it because of this confession. We receive the wisdom and strategy of the Holy Spirit to act—by resisting and fleeing the very appearance of evil. We refuse and we reject the natural inclinations of fallen men.

I decree and declare that we are no longer addicted to anything or anyone worldly or carnal, but we have reversed the curse with our addiction to God's word, His ways, His thoughts, and His plan for our lives. We hear, yield to, and obey the authority of God's word. We are no longer dominated by the world's spirit of error. We welcome, invite and receive the convicting power of the Holy Spirit, and we reject condemnation. We have hearts of true repentance, and sincere change is instant for us. We will not return to the vomit our past. We are witnesses of Who God is, and wherever we go; God's light will be seen upon us. There is no compromise or betrayal in us. We are free from a Judas spirit. We will not deny Him, and He will not deny us.

We are complete in Christ, and our every need is met. We seek no worldly satisfaction because our expectation and hope is in God. My husband, __________ loves himself, therefore he loves me. My wife, _________ respects and loves me as her husband. We both love God with all of our heart, soul, and minds and we love our neighbors as we love ourselves. We are a man and a woman of integrity and mighty in valor (excellence). Daily we are increasing in spiritual prosperity (wisdom, understanding, and knowledge). We have divine favor with God and favor with man. We are empowered to fulfill our God given assignments here on the earth. Our lives of obedience to faith keep us experiencing the fullness of God's blessing. God knows us and calls us His friend because we walk led of the Spirit of God and not by our flesh.

This day, I decree and declare that our deepest desire is to know more of God; to know more of God's love; to know more about His divine grace given to us by our Lord Jesus Christ; and to know more of the fellowship and the sweet communion of the Holy Spirit. My marriage is going from glory to glory, and no demon in hell, agent on the earth, or minister of darkness will stop, block, or hinder our growth in Christ, nor our unity with one another! In Jesus' name. So be it, Amen.

A KING'S PROPHETIC PRAYER OVER HIS/HER CHILDREN

Father God, in the name of Jesus, I thank You, You are our Rock, our Strength, our Fortress, our Deliverer; our God, and our Father; our High Tower, in whom we trust. We come boldly unto the Throne of Grace that we may obtain mercy, and find grace to help in time of need.

I thank You, Lord, for blessing me with the children you have given me (spiritual and natural). The children which the Lord has given me are for signs and wonders from the Lord of Hosts. I decree and declare that no weapon formed against me or my children shall prosper; every tongue that rises against us in judgment will be condemned.

My children are taught of the Lord. Great is their peace. You, Lord, shall keep them in perfect peace, whose mind is stayed on You, because they trust in You. The peace of God, which surpasses all understanding, shall guard their hearts and minds through Christ Jesus.

I thank You, Lord, for:

_ teaching them the fear of the Lord
_ giving them Your judgments and righteousness
_ keeping them back from presumptuous sins
_ giving them beauty, joy, and the garment of praise
_ bestowing mercies and the multitude of Your loving-kindness on them

_ making them wiser than their enemies
_ giving them more understanding than the ancients and their teachers
_ making their enemies at peace with them
_ ordering their steps in Your word
_ letting no iniquity have dominion over them
_ cleansing them from secret sins
_ causing them to hate every false way
_ satisfying them with long life and showing them Your salvation
_ blessing them and enlarging their coasts

Grant unto them your servants that with all boldness they may speak your word.

I decree and declare that my children are kings and priests of the Lord; ministers of our God; the redeemed of the Lord; the holy people; sought out, a city not forsaken; and children that never lie.

My children are like olive plants around the table. They are clothed with the garments of salvation, and covered with the robe of righteousness; they shall eat the riches of the gentiles. Everlasting joy shall be unto them.

All who see them shall acknowledge them; that they are the seed which the Lord hath blessed; they are the heritage of the Lord; they shall never be ashamed. The Spirit of the Lord is upon them, and has anointed them.

I decree and declare that upon my children rests the Spirit of the Lord; the spirit of wisdom and understanding; the spirit of counsel and might; the spirit of knowledge and of the fear of the Lord; and shall make them of quick understanding in the fear of the Lord. They shall not judge after the sight of their eyes, neither reprove at the hearing of their ears; but with righteousness shall they judge.

Thank You, Lord, that there is therefore now no condemnation to my children, who are in Christ Jesus, who walk after the Holy Spirit. For the Law of the Spirit of Life in Christ Jesus has made them free from the law of sin and death.

I decree and declare that my children are strong in the Lord, and in the power of His might. Thank You, Lord, for equipping them with the whole armor of God; that they may be able to stand against the wiles of the devil. Thank You, for equipping them with truth... righteousness; the preparation of the gospel of peace; faith; salvation; and the sword of the Spirit, which is the word of God. I decree and declare that my children bless the Most High, and give no place to the devil; that they submit themselves to God; draw near to God; and humble themselves in the sight of the Lord. I declare that my children:

_ Declare Your faithfulness and salvation
_ Greatly rejoice in the Lord
_ Walk in Truth
_ Walk as children of the light
_ Delight to do your will
_ Are set in a large place by the Lord
_ Are accepted in the Beloved
_ Have a price far above rubies
_ Have the memory of the just

_ Have overcome the spirit of the antichrist
_ Have overcome the world with faith in Jesus Christ
_ Shall never fall
_ Shall ride prosperously
_ Shall rise up and call me blessed
_ Shall never die—they shall live, and declare the works of the Lord

In the name of Jesus, I declare that all bitterness, wrath, anger, malice, clamor, and evil speaking be put away from them. They shall not fulfill the lust of the flesh. They shall not engage in or become victims of adultery; fornication; uncleanness; lasciviousness; idolatry; witchcraft; hatred; variance; emulations; wrath; strife; seditions; heresies; envy; murder; drunkenness; reveling; wickedness; filthy communication; or blasphemy.

I decree and declare that my children have power over all the power of the enemy, and nothing shall by any means hurt them. My children abide in Christ. They shall bear the fruits of the Spirit—love; joy; peace; longsuffering; gentleness; goodness; faith; meekness; and temperance. Thank You, Lord, that my children shall fear You as long as the sun and moon endure—throughout all generations. I thank You for giving them cities great and fenced up to heaven.

_ Prayer shall be made for them continuously
_ All nations shall call them blessed
_ They shall keep the ways of the Lord
_ The words of their mouth and the meditation of their heart are
  acceptable in Your sight

_ God's law is written in their heart and mind
_ God is the strength of their heart and their portion forever
_ Their eyes are lifted up
_ They are lifted up forever

Thank You, Lord, that my children speak the word of God. They shall speak with the enemies at the gate—they shall possess the land. My children and I shall increase more and more. Strength and honor are their clothing. Their mouth is full of the law of kindness and the wisdom of God. Their greatness and comfort are increased by the Lord. They shall open their mouth and speak righteously. They shall defend the cause of the poor and needy.

_ Their calling and election is sure
_ Their names are written in heaven
_ They are sealed with the Holy Spirit of promise

Thank You, Father, in Jesus' name, that goodness and mercy shall follow them all the days of their life, and they shall dwell in the house of the Lord forever. In Jesus' name. Amen.

SPIRITUAL DOMINION FOR PARENTS OF AN ADOPTED CHILD

(Please, for every _______________ add the adopted child's name.)

Father God, in the precious name of Jesus, I declare (adopted child's full name) salvation and I thank You for it. _______________ is born again and spirit-filled! He has been redeemed from the curse of the law! As_______________ legal guardian and parent (spiritual and now natural), I cancel every generational curse from affecting his/her divine destiny that You have ordained for his/her life!

I severe and cut at the root any and all demonic attachments in the spirit realm that would try to claim _______________ destiny illegally! _______________ is free! _______________ is free from the traditions and the demonic spiritual worship of his/her fore-fathers and biological ancestry! _______________ has a new name that is blessed and ordained by the Lord my God and God's hand is on him/her!

I plead the blood of Jesus over_______________ —over his/her body, over the portals of his/her mind, over his/her will and over his/her emotions! I plead the blood of Jesus over his/her destiny! I plead the blood of Jesus over every principality, over every power, over every ruler of darkness in heavenly places assigned against his/her God-given purpose here in the earth!

I decree and declare that the angels of the Lord and the fire of God is protecting and covering _______________ at all times! Therefore, all demonic activity must cease!

I cancel all spirits of demonic inheritance, spirits of generational curses—fear, torment, doubt, anxiety, worry, pain, failure, resistance, irritation, frustration, rejection, loneliness, depression, mistrust, abuse, agitation, and alarm—from dictating _______________ actions and attitudes.

I tear down every stronghold over _______________ life and mind! I bind and I loose _______________ from every demonic soul tie, and loose godly soul ties into and over his/her life! I bind the assignment of all familiar spirits that would try to affiliate or associate with him/her! I release the spirit of love, power, and a sound mind upon _______________. I release the spirit of peace, boldness, spiritual mindedness, liberty, and courage upon _______________. He/she is not afraid of the terror by night, nor of the demonic arrows that fly by day (Psalm 91:5).

_______________ spiritual eyes and ears are open clearly to hear and obey God's voice and the voice of his spiritual and legal guardians. He/she follows the voice of the Good Shepherd, but the voice of a stranger he/she will not follow!_______________ understands and recognizes the "Blessing" that is upon him/her, and he/her appreciates his/her new life in Christ and his/her new life with his/her ordained parents.

I release the intimacy of relationship with the Lord Jesus upon ________! I decree and I declare that ________ inner self thirsts and yearns for God and that he/she will see God's face! So be it.

REBUKE MIGHTY NATIONS THAT HINDERS PROSPERITY

A Personal Journal Entry

Saturday, March 16, 2013—7:30

Led this morning to receive the Lord driving out nations that are wicked that I may possess their land. While praying (warring) in the Spirit I was led to Deuteronomy 7:1 to rebuke nations greater and mightier—the seven evil spirits that war against the saints and the divine will of God for their lives—the Hittites, the Girgashites, the Amorites, the Canaanites, the Perizzites, the Hivites and the Jebusites (seven nations) . . . Here is what I spoke and you can declare as well:

Father, in the majestic name of Jesus I receive the Lord my God driving out nations (challenges, obstacles, bondages, hindrances, and set traps) mightier and greater than me. I receive the wicked driven out before me that I may possess all the promises of my God. I rebuke every Hittite—Babylonian characteristic and the spirit of fear. I come against and bind all sons, spirits of terror, deceit, mind torment, phobia, depression, and oppression! I rebuke every Girgashite—carnal, earthly, clay dwelling, and unbelief spirit.

I rebuke every Amorite spirit that would try to cause me to focus on mountains instead of speaking to them and removing them by faith. I am not obsessed with earthly fame—I seek the glory of God! I rebuke every Canaanite—addictive, addiction, perverted, exaggerated, and people pleasing spirit—from operating in me or against me. I bind every Perizzite—blood sucking, time stealing, destiny devouring, low self-esteem, lazy, vision-less spirit—in Jesus' name! I speak to every Hivite (village, comfortable, complacent) spirit and every Jebusite spirit (controlling, minimizer of destiny and spiritual authority that I have as a believer), and I rebuke you from suppressing my God-given kingship and rightful inheritance as an heir of God and a joint heir with Christ.

Greater is He that is in me than he that is in the world! I receive the wealth of these seven wicked nations. I receive great and goodly cities which I did not build, houses full of all good things which I did not fill . . . olive trees which I did not plant. I receive the wealth of the wicked nations. I receive its release into my hands and into the hands of the Church.

I'm reminded to never forget the Lord my God, for it is He that has given me the power to get wealth. Not because of my righteousness, but because He made a promise to my forefathers Abraham, Isaac, and Jacob. I thank You, Lord, for giving me the word to pray and the words to say to fully experience the blessing of being your child—a son of God, and the seed of Abraham. Glory, glory, glory! I love You.

Deuteronomy 9:5
Deuteronomy 7:1
Deuteronomy 6:10–12
Deuteronomy 8:17–20

POVERTY WILL NO LONGER FIND ME

"Do not love sleep, lest you come to poverty; Open your eyes and you will be satisfied with bread."

~ *Proverbs 20:13 NKJV*

I **rise early to pray** . . . I decree and declare that poverty will no longer find me! Wealth, riches, honor, and the glory that God has for me here in the earth shall find me! I receive them in the name of Jesus! I decree and declare that my life is balanced—spirit, soul, body and financially! My finances are lining up right now in divine order! God will truly receive the glory through me in every area of my life from this moment forward!

I walk uprightly, I seek the Lord and I fear Him . . . no good thing will the Lord withhold from me! I receive the fruit and the increase of the earth! The earth is the Lord's and the fullness (fruitfulness) of it. The Lord my God is in me, therefore, the earth is mine as well, and the fruit of it! Therefore, I receive His inheritance here in the earth as a good steward until He returns. I am His representative in Christ, and I receive all that is His. I am God's heir and a joint heir with Jesus . . . what belongs to Him belongs to me. He has authorized my stewardship and I receive it! I have the privilege of benefiting from what belongs to Him as a joint heir. I am a king in His Kingdom, and I take my position gratefully! When I speak, the earth responds, and the angels ascend and descend according to the words that I speak.

Because I love the Lord and I obey His word to love Him, to love myself, and to love my neighbor, He has made His home in me. He won't settle for less, and neither will I! I am mindful that, upon His return, I will come to my true expected inheritance . . . salvation, redemption and the opportunity to live in the new earth where there is no trace of poverty! My true inheritance is life beyond what I see right now. My mind and my heart are set on this, so that I will not depart nor deny the Lord as my wealth, riches, honor, and glory increase here in this earth. I remain thankful to You, Father, for true riches to come that give me hope beyond my imagination. I love You.

But for now, Lord, I expect to experience heaven on earth. I am seated in heavenly places in Christ, and I expect to experience His lifestyle. I expect from You, God, and You alone. I expect Your presence daily! I expect Your manifested glory daily! I expect Your grace to rest upon me abundantly that I may give and bless others the way I desire to—the way You desire for me to. Thank You for heaven in the earth through me. I have entered this day boldly to the throne of grace to obtain mercy and to find grace to help in a time of need. In Jesus' name I believe and I know I receive!

I am a king and a priest unto the Lord! My life (spirit, soul, body, and financially) is evidence of who I am in Christ here in the earth! I decree and declare that the whole creation can see that I am a son of God. So be it!

"Let the peoples praise You, O God; Let all the peoples praise You. Then the earth shall yield her increase; God, our own God, shall bless us. God shall bless us, and all the ends of the earth shall fear Him."

~ Psalms 67:5–7 NKJV

A PROMISE FOR SEED SOWERS

A Year Crowned with an Abundant Harvest

December 25, 2010 ~ *TLW*

Rain has been pouring and pouring down for at least 5 or more days. Each day the Lord would lead me to particular scriptures early in the morning. I received great understanding that the natural rain began in the spirit realm first and there was great significance to be shared through His word. I believe if you are reading this, these words of life will encourage you to keep doing what you are doing—keep sowing seed. The law of faith is working on your behalf—that God will be exalted through you.

Saturday, December 18th 6:51am (Rain in its Season)

"I give rain in its season." "Yes, Lord. I receive rain in my season—which is now!"

> "The Lord will open to you His good treasure, the heavens, to give the rain to your land in its season, and to bless all the work of your hand. You shall lend to many nations, but you shall not borrow."
>
> ~ *Deuteronomy 28:12*

Tuesday, December 22nd around 3 or 4am (Rain—Souls)

"Keep interceding and praying for the lost. Keep sowing My word into their hearts. They need it—it's theirs just as much as it's yours. This is seed that is also sown toward an abundant harvest—My harvest of souls. Get me Mine—I will see to it that you get yours." Yes, Lord.

This particular morning the rain was coming down very hard—not common—I could literally hear young voices screaming and crying—I was wide awake—I prayed in the spirit immediately in intercession.

Tuesday, December 22nd PM (God's Thoughts—Rain)

> "For as the rain and snow come down from the heavens, and return not there again, but water the earth and make it bring forth and sprout, that it may give seed to the sower and bread to the eater.
>
> So shall My Word be that goes forth out of My mouth: it shall not return to Me void (without producing any effect, useless), but it shall accomplish that which I please and purpose, and it shall prosper in the thing for which I sent it."
>
> ~ *Isaiah 55:10, 11 Amp.*

Friday, December 24th 8am (The Rain Stopped)

Reminded of the following scripture before I was led to the rest:

> "Rise up you women who are at ease! Hear my voice, you confident and careless daughters! Listen to what I am saying (to you)!"
>
> ~ *Isaiah 32:9 Amp.*

I read on actually seeking some more words of encouragement due to the conviction of being too comfortable as mentioned in the previous verse. I was happily led by the Spirit of the Lord to this powerful verse, being mindful that the natural rain had ceased . . .

> "Happy and fortunate are you who cast your seed upon all waters (when the river overflows its banks; for the seed will sink into the mud and when the waters subside, the plant will spring up; you will find it after many days and reap an abundant harvest), you who safely send forth . . . freely."
>
> ~ *Isaiah 32:20 Amp.*

The word "will" is a promise made by God—not man—He cannot lie and His word will not return void.

> "Blessed (happy, fortunate, prosperous, and enviable) is the man who walks and lives not in the counsel of the ungodly (following after their advice, their plans and purposes), nor stands (submissive and inactive) in the path where sinners walk, nor sits down (to relax and rest) where the scornful (and the mockers) gather.
>
> But his delight and desire are in the law of the Lord, and on His law (the precepts, the instructions, the teachings of God) he habitually meditates (ponders and studies) by day and by night.
>
> And he shall be like a tree firmly planted (and tended) by the streams of water, ready to bring forth its fruit in its season; its leaf

> also shall not fade or wither, and everything he does shall prosper (and come to maturity)."
>
> ~ *Psalms 1:1–3 Amp.*

God is exalted as we prosper.

> "The Lord is exalted, for He dwells on high; he will fill Zion with justice and righteousness (moral and spiritual rectitude in every area and relation).
>
> And there shall be stability in your times, an abundance of salvation, wisdom, and knowledge; the reverent fear and worship of the Lord is your treasure and His."
>
> ~ *Isaiah 33:5, 6 Amp.*

People will see evidence that you are saved by your prosperity. Prosperity spirit, soul, body, emotionally, relationally, and financially.

Your year has been crowned with an abundant harvest from all the seed that you have sown—His word and His money that He has blessed you with. Do not sleep through your harvest. Its harvest time and you will see it in many days. Keep on sowing—something great is working on your behalf. If you don't stop—it won't stop. Let it rain.

> "You crown the year with a bountiful harvest; even the hard pathways overflow with abundance."
>
> ~ *Psalm 65:11(NLT)*

SUPERNATURAL DEBT CANCELLATION

There failed no part of any good thing which the Lord had promised to the house of Israel; all came to pass.

~*Joshua 21:45*

Father Your word says in **Isaiah 66:8** NKJV, "Who has heard such a thing? Who has seen such things? Shall the earth be made to give birth in one day? Or shall a nation be born at once . . . ?"

We declare debt cancellation in one day for our ministry, the house of the Lord at (name of ministry), and for our homes in Jesus' name! We know by faith that Your word will not return void! We know that You are the same miracle working God as you were in the times past! You are the same yesterday, today, and forevermore! We declare and we receive a financial miracle as we commit all financial matters to You. We commit them to Your truth, to Your righteousness, and to the counsel of Your word!

We are a tithing, sowing ministry, and we support missionaries nationwide and globally. As we continue to do our part—from pure hearts—we know Your promise is already done. We thank You in advance for the manifestation. By the same faith as Abraham, Isaac, Jacob and Jesus our Lord we receive supernatural debt cancellation. Amen, so be it.

By faith we understand that the worlds (during the successive ages) were framed (fashioned, put in order, and equipped for their

Hebrews 11
Isaiah 55:11
Isaiah 66:8

intended purpose) by the word of God, so that what we see was not made out of things which are visible.

~ *Hebrews 11:3*

THE BLESSINGS OF OBEDIENCE

Father, in the name of Jesus, I **diligently** (on purpose) obey Your voice and I observe carefully all Your commandments which You command me this day. I decree and I declare that **I have been set high above** all the nations of the earth, and all these blessings are coming upon me and overtaking me because I obey the voice of the Lord my God.

I am **blessed** in this city! I am **blessed** in this country! I am **blessed** in the Inland Empire (or your city)! I am **blessed** in my house! I am **blessed** in my marriage! I am **blessed** in my serving! **Blessed** is the fruit of my body (I am fruitful), and the produce of my ground (my territory), and the increase of my herds (my disciples), and the increase of my bank accounts, and the increase of my investments, and the increase of the revelation that God has given me! Blessed am I when I come in—**everywhere**! Blessed am I when I go out—**everywhere!**

The Lord has caused my enemies (the enemy of debt—the enemy of poverty—the enemy of deficiency—the enemy of living paycheck to paycheck—the enemy of wrong relationships—the enemy that would try to come against my soul)to be defeated before my face! They will come out against me one way and flee before me seven ways! I am prospering! My God, the Lord, **has commanded His Blessing** on my storehouses, on my ministry, on my bank accounts, on my investments, on my relationships, on my health. To **all that I set my hand to**, the Lord has commanded His blessing upon it! The Lord has blessed me in the land that He has given me. The Lord has established me as a holy person to Him, as I keep the commandments of the Lord my God—and walk—and talk in His ways. ALL the peoples of this earth they see me and they call me by the name of the Lord, and they are afraid of me!

The Lord has granted me plenty of goods—the fruit of my body, the increase of ALL (my produce—my products, my accounts, my spirit, my soul, my body, my relationships). ALL that I put my hand to, the Lord has increased it! And the Lord has opened to me His good treasury—**The Heavens**! To give me rain in my season—which is now! This is my season, and He has blessed the work of my hand. I shall lend to many nations, but I will not borrow! The Lord has made me, and I walk in this—I am the head and not the tail, I am **above only** and not beneath, as I heed the commandments of the Lord my God which I have been commanded! **I have been commanded to increase in Faith** by adding to my Faith—virtue, integrity, character, knowledge, self-control, perseverance, patience, endurance, godliness, brotherly-kindness, and LOVE! **I add love on a daily basis** because I am commanded by the Lord to do so.

This keeps me experiencing the blessing of the Lord that is upon me. I will not turn aside from any of the words that are written in the book of law (the word of God)! I will not turn to the right or to the left. And should I make a mistake, I will repent **quickly** understanding that my God forgives and He forgets. He reminds me to keep confessing His word—

His Blessing that has made me rich and has added no sorrow to my life! I will go after no other god(s) but You, God, and serve You and You alone. —**The Blessing is my lifestyle!** So be it.

Deuteronomy 28:1–14
2 Peter 1:5–7

A KINGS ENEMIES DEFEATED

> He allowed no man to do them wrong; in fact, He reproved kings for their sakes, saying, touch not My anointed, and do My prophets no harm.
>
> ~ *Psalms 105:14–15*

Father God, I receive and I thank You in advance for the defeat of every one of my enemies and accusers!

Thank You for silencing, subduing and abolishing the enemy and the avenger on my behalf. I receive ordained strength because of my enemies. I am saved from my enemies and from the hand of all that hate me. I am delivered out of the hands of my enemies and I serve God without fear. I love my enemies. I bless them and do them good only. I pray for those that despitefully use me and persecute me. As a result, my reward is great . . . I receive.

No weapon formed against me can prosper. Every lying tongue that rises against me I will show to be wrong. God is for me. No one and no thing—no power, no principality, no spiritual host of wickedness, and no darkness—can be against me or defeat me. The Lord is my Avenger, He is the Avenger of all things. The Lord fights my every battle. The victory is already mine! Praise God! I cast the care of any battle to the

Lord. I am one with Him and He cares for me. It's already done. It's already won.

I give thanksgiving, Father, for the victory. I reign with my Lord Jesus . . . I declare that every enemy of this world system and in the heavens above are under our feet! In Jesus' name. Amen. So be it.

> If the world hates you, know that it hated Me before it hated you. If you belonged to the world the world would treat you with affection and would love you as its own. But because you are not of the world (no longer one with it), but I have chosen (selected) you out of the world, the world hates (detests) you.
>
> ~*John 15:18–19*

John 15:18-19
Isaiah 54:17
Psalms 8:2
Matthew 5:44
Luke 1:71, 74
Luke 6:35
1 Thessalonians 4:6

CHAPTER

CORPORATE MINISTRY RELATED (FOR INTERCESSORS OF A MINISTRY)

The title of this chapter says it all. These are strategic prayers that will assist the intercessor of a family or a church home to bring divine order in a meeting, worship service, fellowship, and or a corporate outreach outing. A few are targeted to acquiring land and financial wealth—all of which the Body of Believers need to see the glory of God manifested to the world.

WORSHIP SERVICE OPENING PRAYER

Father God, we take this opportunity to commit our service(s) into Your charge and into Your care. We receive the ministry of the Holy Spirit. We welcome the Spirit of Truth. We declare Your blessing upon all that will take place.

Thank You for evidence of Your anointing. Thank You for evidence of Your manifested presence. Thank You for evidence of Your love. Thank You for evidence of Your power and of Your glory. We are sure to give You all the praise and all the honor.

We thank You in advance that every need is met. Those who need to make a decision today will choose life, receive forgiveness of sins, and receive their inheritance among the saints in light.

Satan we rebuke you! We give you no place in this house. We cancel every evil assignment against the hearts and the minds of the people. We bind all distractions. We declare the word of God will go forth unhindered and unchecked by any and all outside forces. God's word will not fail. It will be confirmed with signs following.

We receive the spirit of wisdom and revelation in the knowledge of You, God. We declare that every ear and heart is open and ready to receive.

We thank You for our pastor and prophet, (say pastor's name). We thank You for the truth that will be delivered by the demonstration of the Holy Spirit and of power. We thank You for words and wisdom from heaven downloaded into each and every one of our hearts.

Thank You in advance for increase. Thank You for multiplication. Thank You for the new victories and the sincere change we will all experience today as a result of Your word, and as a result of Your burden removing, yoke destroying power! In Jesus' name we pray. Amen, so be it.

PRE-SERVICE INTERCESSION/WARFARE VICTORY

> And I also say to you that you are Peter, and on this rock I will build My church, and the gates of Hades shall not prevail against it. And I will give you the keys of the kingdom of heaven, and whatever you bind on earth will be bound in heaven, and whatever you loose on earth will be loosed in heaven.
>
> ~*Matthew 16:18–19 NKJV*

*As the assigned prayer leader(s) pray the prayers below and all who are in attendance should pray lightly in the spirit.

A. Commit services and all activity "pre," "during," and "post" into God's charge and care. Commit both those who will hear and those who will speak to God as well. Declare the lordship of Jesus Christ upon the grounds and welcome the ministry of the Holy Spirit to flow throughout.

   Declare, "We take authority over our service(s) being held!" Decree and declare that the gates of hell will not prevail against the church—specifically not against this house!" Bind every work of the flesh from prospering or drawing attention to itself!

B. Bind the work of all witches and warlocks and shut their mouths with this command:

"We cancel every cursed word spoken through witches and warlocks. We cancel any and all spells, hexes, works of divination, and bewitchment sent to oppose us or come against the divine order of God for this house! We declare the anointing of God will immediately destroy spirits of oppression, depression, lust and perversion, interruptions and all trickery. We announce in Jesus' name that all assignments of the enemy are incapable of harming us!"

C. Declare that no weapon will form or prosper during the service(s):

"We plead the blood of Jesus over every aspect of the service(s)—from the people, to the word, to the finances, to the ends of the campus grounds, and over the sanctuary. Satan we bind you and every principality, power, ruler of darkness, and spiritual host of wickedness in heavenly places. We bind every evil spirit, every demon spirit, every Jezebel spirit, and every spirit of Belial. We bind every adulteress, seductive spirit. We bind all these demon spirit's assignments that would try to test, tempt, distract, hinder, or come against any of us or those coming through the sanctuary doors in Jesus' name!"

D. Bind every work of the flesh that would try to distract or oppose the will and the work of God from going forth. Declare this time set—a divine appointment from God Himself.

Bind any strongmen that would try to blind the eyes and ears of the hearer from receiving all that God will release through the Pastor.

Bind all distractions and confusion during the altar call. Declare the removal of any veils that would hide the gospel from any person present or that may hear the teaching through means of media. Declare lives changed as a result of God's word shared.

E. Bind all queen spirits and goddess spirits. Bind all familiar spirits—spirits of flattery and manipulation from approaching the greeting and receiving lines of the leaders with their own agendas. Cancel those interactions that are not sent by God.

   Bind all shade tree preaching and spirits of divination from causing distractions during the delivery of the word of God. Bind the spirit of rebellion from rising up in any ministry of helps going forth. Bind spirits that usurp and resist authority. Bind spirits that would resist the Truth and bind the opinions of men from being released throughout the congregation. Loose the wisdom of God to prevail.

F. Bind all spirits of religion from contaminating true "real" servants of the Lord. Bind all operations of Pharisee, religious spirits. Bind the spirit of error and release or loose the Spirit of Truth to prevail.

   Bind the spirits of pride and arrogance that would try to take root in the hearts of the believers. Loose the spirit of humility and the fear of the Lord upon all. Bind all subcultures inside the house. Declare that all are of the same mind, doing the same, and all are obedient to the counsel and wisdom of God.

   Declare that all are under God-given authority, serving God (and others) with joy and gladness of heart. Bind all kingdoms attempting to operate in or through the ministry that are not the kingdom of God.

G. Bind all technical difficulties in Jesus' name! Declare that every taping, recording, and distribution of product will be done without hindrance or hiccups.

Bind all spirits contrary to the spirit of excellence. Tear down strongholds and cast down every vain thought and wicked imagination in the church that would try to exalt itself against the knowledge of God! Bind every mind, thought, action, and will to the will and purpose of God for this house.

Declare that any kingdoms of this world (that would try to position themselves) in this house or in the Body of Christ have become the kingdoms of our God! Declare that they are bowing down right now and that Jesus is exalted and magnified at all times.

H. Loose the fruit of the Spirit. Loose love, joy, peace, longsuffering, kindness, goodness, faithfulness, gentleness, and self-control to operate in the lives of all involved. Ensure that God receives all the glory through the ministry of the Holy Spirit.

Loose the spirit of a true worshipper—from the choir stands, to the sanctuary chairs, and to those seated in them!

Loose the ministry of love. Loose the spirit of compassion.

I. Release the garment of praise for the spirit of heaviness. Release the 'true' spirit of thanksgiving. Loose the ability to discern between good and evil. Loose the ability to discern between true sheep and false sheep. Loose the ability to discern between the wolves and the goats—those sent to draw the Church out of faith and out of obedience to the order of the house of the Lord.

Loose the heart of God to replace every stony, unbelieving, and doubting heart. Declare that great works will be done in the house. Release the supernatural on every operating natural area.

J. Loose the spirit of peace. Declare that peace is being still right now! Loose great faith in the house. Release the spirit of expectation. Release the reverential fear of the Lord upon the Church. Release an 'on time', punctual spirit to operate in the house.

   Loose the mind of Christ in the house of the Lord. Declare that all think like, act like, live like, and talk like God! Release a single eye focus. Declare that every eye is single in the congregation and that the entire body is filled with light—revelation from God.

K. Loose into each and every person's life the anointing of God to remove any burdens and to destroy any yokes. Loose the word of God in every person's mind, mouth, and heart that God's kingdom will reign and dominate on the earth through us. Declare that all are yielding right now to the fruit of the Spirit and mortifying every deed of the flesh. Declare that the gifts of the Spirit are flowing freely through the church and every house of the Lord to set the captives free and edify the Church.

L. Receive the Lord Jesus in advance. Receive a great manifestation of His glory. Give thanks for the Spirit of Truth—Who will lead all in the ministry and as individuals into all truth—this day and night season. Declare every need met. Receive any and all angelic assistance, in Jesus' name!

Assuredly, I say to you, whatever you bind on earth will be bound in heaven, and whatever you loose on earth will be loosed in heaven. Again I say to you that if two of you agree on earth concerning anything that they ask, it will be done for them by My Father in heaven. For where two or three are gathered together in My name, I am there in the midst of them.

~ *Matthew 18:18–20 NKJV*

BINDING OF MOCKERS AND SCORNERS

> Now therefore do not be scoffers, lest the bands which bind you be made strong; for a decree of destruction have I heard from the Lord God of hosts upon the whole land *and* the whole earth.
>
> ~ *Isaiah 28:22*

In Jesus' name we bind all persecutors, soothsayers, scorners, mockers, liars, gossipers, and un-checked evil doers. We bind the spirit of error and loose the Spirit of Truth. We drive any infection of these spirits out of the house of the Lord at (ministry name).

We declare the mouth of every negative seed sown is shut and closed. We declare these seeds powerless. Every word that the Heavenly Father has not planted in the minds and the hearts of the believers is cursed right now at the root. We replace these negative seeds sown with words of life and the truth concerning this house.

Our harvest is now—uncontaminated and unhindered by any witchcraft, rebellion, hate, jealousy, envy, strife, division, and sorcery. In Jesus' name, so be it.

> They told you beforehand, In the last days (in the end time) there will be scoffers [who seek to gratify their own unholy desires], following after their own ungodly passions.
>
> ~ *Jude 1:18*

BEFORE CORPORATE/COMMUNITY OUTREACH

A. Father God, in the powerful name of Jesus, we commit taking the altar to the community to You! We commit this outreach effort into Your care and charge. We commit it to your word and the power of the Holy Spirit!

We ask, Father, for Your blessing upon this corporate outreach—understanding that it is not by our might, nor is it by our power, that we go—but it is by the Spirit of the Lord and faith!

Holy Spirit; we commit and come under Your lordship. We put our bodies under subjection and mortify any deeds of our flesh. We fully understand that this is Your ministry, and we humble ourselves as co-laborers with You.

Holy Spirit, we ask that You send God's love, His healing, and His reconciling power before us that will bring restoration to all to whom we come in contact with today.

As we go by faith, we decree and declare that the love of God will be evident and tangible. We decree and declare that everyone with whom we have a divine appointment in this day will be met right where they are they will come to know Jesus in a practical way that is real and personal to them.

B. Thank You, Father, that You have opened the doors of utterance for us to preach the good news of the gospel to the nations of the earth. You have granted us favor in the eyes of all residents, home owners, management teams, store owners, and the law enforcement personnel.

We thank You Father that we preach and teach Your word with boldness—in the demonstration of the Spirit and of power—that every yoke is destroyed, and every burden removed by the anointing of God.

We thank You, Father, for signs and wonders that will take place—that the lame will walk; the blind will see; the diseased are cleansed; the dead are raised; the demon possessed are set free; and the gospel is preached to the poor. We heal the broken hearted; preach deliverance to the captives; cause recovery of sight to the blind; set at liberty them that are bruised; and preach the acceptable year of the Lord!

We go forth doing good, as commanded, and healing all who are oppressed by the devil!

C. We declare the freedom of all nations that have been in bondage to the powers of darkness (witchcraft, sorcery, bewitchment, false religion, idolatry, queen spirit worship, famine and drought, poverty, slavery to their past & present, terrorism, oppression, depression and spiritual adultery). We decree and declare that the refugees are freed, in Jesus' name.

We thank You, Father, that today those that sit in darkness shall see a great light. We are the salt of the earth, and we are that great light.

The lost shall come to Your light that rests upon us, receive forgiveness of sins, and receive their inheritance among the saints in light.

Father, we ask that You turn their wilderness into a Garden of Eden. Restore any years of devastation suffered while they were under the curse, and cause them to marvel, knowing that through their covenant with You, Father, they were the last, but now they are the first!

D. We understand that Jesus could do no great works in His own hometown due to their unbelief. So we take the authority right now and we bind, rebuke and cast out any spirits of fear, worry, doubt, anxiety, and unbelief, and give them no place in our lives, nor in the lives of those that we will minister to. We rebuke the spirit of fear in Jesus' name! Each and every one of us operate in the spirit of power, love and a sound mind!

We pull down all strongholds and cast down every vain and wicked imagination that would try to exalt itself against the knowledge of God and we bring our every thought captive to the obedience of Christ. We declare that we have the mind of Christ—His thoughts and purpose is ours!

We loose the spirit of great faith, confidence and boldness to rest upon us that mighty works will be done in our hometown, community, and surrounding cities.

We will fulfill the greater works that we have been called to accomplish in this day!

E. As gospel ambassadors, as ministers of reconciliation, and as perfect laborers, no man shall lay a hand on us. We decree and declare that the angels of the Lord are encamped around about us to protect us and deliver us from all evil, and that the fire of God protects us and covers us. We are fearless in the face of adversity, and You, Father, have given us a mouth—words and wisdom that the enemy cannot gainsay nor resist. We exercise wisdom, discretion, and sound judgment at all times.

Thank you, Father, for the spirit of wisdom and knowledge in the revelation of You and Your will. We declare that the Spirit of wisdom, the Spirit of understanding, the Spirit of knowledge, the Spirit of divine counsel, the Spirit of supernatural might, and the utmost fear of the Lord is resting upon us right now, in Jesus' name!

F. As brothers and sisters in Christ, we are strong in the Lord and in the power of His might! We place upon ourselves the full armor of God—that we may be able to stand against the strategies of the devil. We understand that we are not wrestling with flesh and blood, but against principalities, against powers, against the rulers of the darkness of this world, against spiritual wickedness in high places.

Therefore, we put on God's complete armor that we may be able to stand in this evil day, and when we have done all to stand, we will keep on standing out in the mission field. The belt of truth is tight around our waist. We put on the breastplate of righteous. Our feet are shod with the preparation of the gospel of peace, and we are ever ready to share the good news!

Above all, we take the shield of faith which will quench every fiery dart and flaming missile of the wicked one. We take the helmet of salvation, and the sword of the Spirit—which is the word of God. The Glory of God is our rear guard.

As well, we pray in the spirit always (all the time and on every occasion) being watchful and alert with strong purpose . . . interceding on behalf of God consecrated people.

We receive the freedom of utterance so that we may open our mouths boldly to proclaim the mystery of the good news of the gospel—for which we are ambassadors, declaring it boldly and courageously as we ought to!

G. Finally, Father, we give thanks to You for what has already been done, and for the privilege to serve You and others in Your kingdom. We thank you for the opportunity to see the work of Your hand, and for the honor to walk in the good works set forth before time.

We thank You for the hearts You have already prepared, and the souls You have already declared won in this day. We thank You for those who will believe that they will be baptized in the name of Jesus—with the evidence of speaking in another tongue (their heavenly language). We thank You for immediate answered prayers, and for signs, miracles, and wonders that will confirm your word!

We thank You for choosing each and every one of us as vessels in the ministry of the Holy Spirit here in the earth. We covet every gift of the Spirit of God, and say have Your way with us, Holy Spirit. May Your gifts edify the church and set the captives free!

We thank You, Father, for a toil free day of corporate outreach, and for the new victories that come with it. We are sure to give You, and You alone, all the glory! In Jesus' name we pray. Amen.

PRAYER AFTER CORPORATE/COMMUNITY OUTREACH

A. By faith, we take this opportunity to commit to God all the souls we have ministered to (say their *full* names out loud) . . . in Jesus' name. We deposit them into God's charge and care. We entrust them to God's protection. We commend them to the word of His grace—to the commands, counsels, and promises of His unmerited favor.

We declare that they are now disciples for Christ. Father God, teach them personally Your word, and Your ways. Increase Your wisdom in them and through them. Father, thank You for causing them to know You and our Lord Jesus as one—just as we are one with You. Thank You for keeping them from the evil one and sanctifying them with Your truth.

May they experience sweet communion with the Holy Spirit and live lives that are pleasing in Your sight full of power and obedience to Your word. We declare that they are not only hearers but doers of the word. Holy Spirit, administer the love of God and the grace of our Lord Jesus to each of them. Thank You for filling any voids in their hearts that would attempt to cause them to draw back from the word of faith they have received.

We pray that their faith will not fail and that they will remain strengthened in the word of God daily through personal study, and by the changing power of the Holy Spirit working in and through them.

B. We plead the blood of Jesus over each and every one of them. We cancel every demonic attack of the enemy from forming or prospering against them. We bind all false teachers, false prophets, and false apostles from speaking words that are contrary to the word of God that has been sown into their hearts.

We cancel the cares of the world from choking and stealing the word of God. We declare the word of God—the seed that is now in their hearts—will not fail. It's increasing right now! The seed shall remain and bear much fruit. The seed sown will only grow and multiply causing them to know God intimately. We declare that they will continue to experience God's presence like never before—personally for themselves. The seed will cause them to go and make disciples, just like us.

Father, thank You for ordering their steps. May they be at the right place at the right time, with the right words of life, and the right people. We declare them trees of righteousness! By faith they are firmly planted in the Lord's vineyard. Nothing and no one will pluck them up! *They are the planting of the Lord* and will remain in the kingdom of God. They love God and they serve God with all of their hearts in truth, in holiness, and in righteousness.

We declare the salvations (manifested today) broke generational curses! New kings entered the kingdom of God, redeemed their family bloodline from the curse of Adam and received the blessing of Abraham! From this day forward we declare a new generation of Jesus worshippers with them and as a result of them!

C. Those reached today will come and receive the complete purpose of God for their lives in the house of the Lord at (say ministry name). May they see and experience the advantages and benefits of salvation combined with the power of the Holy Spirit! We declare divine deliverance daily for each and every one of them from any bondages that would try to call them back from the faith that they have received. We bind and loose the spirit of fear and cancel its attempt to capture their minds. We loose the spirit of power, the spirit of love, and the spirit of a sound mind upon them.

We declare that every outreach card, prayer booklet or ministry track placed or given all contain words of life. They will reap the life of thirsty souls coming to learn more of Jesus and more about life in Christ. Father, thank You in advance for reminding them of this visitation from You. Draw them to where the candle is lit and where the Bible is taught soundly at (say ministry name). We call our harvest in right now into our house of worship! Our labor is not in vain. We will see the fruit it. We receive the increase God that only You can bring as a result of the word watered and sown. If they are from another country or state, help them to find Your assigned house of worship.

Father, thank You once again for the opportunity to co-labor with Christ! We ask that You anoint us with a fresh anointing, as well as the grace needed to do follow ups effectively—causing continued discipleship and the display of Your love.

We also receive Your rewards Father, for those who win souls. We receive wisdom. We receive time redeemed. We receive assured answered prayer in Jesus' name! We love You, Father God. We love You, Lord Jesus. We love You, Holy Spirit! Thank You for sending us. Amen, so be it.

Acts 20:32–33
John 17

D. **Pray in the spirit 5–10 minutes.** Allow the Holy Spirit to have the final words over the destiny of those ministered to.

TAKING POSSESSION OF LAND PROMISED

Father God, we boldly come before Your throne of grace as heirs of God and joint heirs with Jesus to receive and take possession (in the spirit-realm and in the earth-realm) our land promised, (address of property). As kings, in Your kingdom we operate in the authority, dominion, and power that You have given us to take it by force! It's our inheritance; we claim it and receive it, in Jesus' name! It is the Lord our God who has brought us into the land which we are possessing. As our avenger God, we believe You have already cast out nations greater and mightier than us from our territory!

We bind the strongman that has held this property in captivity, and we evict every evil spirit in its' sphere of influence that would try to threaten or hinder its' release in Jesus' name! For Your word says, Father, that, "Every place that the sole of our foot will tread upon I have given you . . ." The land is ours, and what God has already done in heaven no man or power here in the earth or heavenlies can undo it! Not one thing has failed of all the good things which the Lord our God has spoken concerning (name of ministry). **All have come to pass for us; not one word has failed!** For the Lord has given us a land that we did not have to labor for, (a city that we did not have to build), and we shall dwell in it!

We plead the blood of Jesus over every principality, power, ruler of darkness, and spiritual wickedness in high places assigned against the purpose of God for the ministry of (name of ministry). We decree and declare that this prayer is disrupting dark plans right now and giving our enemies a non-prosperous day! We send confusion to the tongues of all who would speak against God's perfect will for our second location of fellowship and worship!

We bind every false representative of Christ connected to the (name of ministry). We bind all spirits that operate contrary to the promise of God for us to take possession! We bind all soothsayers! We bind all spirits that would cause people to slander, rebel, cause division or discord, or to speak against what God has done and is doing! We bind all spirits of fear, doubt, and unbelief! We break all powers of the spirit of heaviness that would try to sap our confidence and trust in the Lord, as we move forward boldly taking what belongs to us! We are free from negative emotions, and quitting is not an option in our lives! We boldly take possession of the land promised as a portion of our rightful inheritance!

The divine favor of God is upon the ministry of (name of ministry), and we expect doors to remain open. We expect special privileges to the point that it is noticeable, and we expect divine advantages to be released on our behalf. We have favor with all who play an important role in the process of our taking possession of (address of property). Devil, any time that has been stolen in this process of eviction and possession we declare is returned to us sevenfold! We are on God's divine timetable and His calendar!

Every member and partner of (name of ministry) has thinking that lines up with the perfect will of God and His agenda for our ministry. We cancel any demonic or evil thought patterns designed that are contrary!

As Ambassador's of Christ in the most powerful institution in the world (the Church), we stand together as a mighty force—praying always and at all times in the Spirit; being watchful and alert to the end—with all perseverance, endurance, and determination—until and beyond the day that the keys are released to our new place of worship! **We thank and praise You daily, Father**, for what You have done. Multitudes will be blessed and set free as a result! So be it, in Jesus' name! Amen!

DECLARATION OF BUDGET MET

> And my God will liberally supply (fill to the full) your every need according to His riches in glory in Christ Jesus. To our God and Father be glory forever and ever (through the endless eternities of the eternities). Amen (so be it).
>
> ~ *Philippians 4:19–20*

We decree and declare that the *daily, monthly,* and *yearly* budget of our ministry (name) has been met! As a ministry in the move of the Holy Spirit, we decree and declare that we live in God's provision! We are not of this world neither are we of this world's system! Holy Spirit, Spirit of Truth, we receive Your announcing and declaring to us the things that are to come. We receive the disclosing and the transmittal of what is the Father's to us. For You are our Teacher, and we ask that You continue to teach us to profit!

Father, we know that it is You that has given us the power to get wealth that You may establish Your covenant that You swore to our forefathers, as it is this day. By the power that works in us, we use the word of Faith to declare Your precious promises calling them from Heaven to the earth!

We thank You Father that You take pleasure and that You are delighted in our prosperity. Your word declares that, as we walk uprightly and trust in

You, we will continue to lack no good thing. We seek the kingdom of God and His righteous here at (ministry name) and all other things are being added to us—right now!

We decree and declare that the wealth anointing is upon us. When we sow seed there is no time before the harvest appears! The harvest is now, immediate, and greatly increased on our behalf! We thank You Father that You have crowned our year with goodness and our paths drip with Your abundance! For You, Lord have blessed this house. We are filled with the uncompromisingly righteous and You have surrounded us with Your favor as a shield. Thank You. We have high expectations of experiencing Your good now and continually!

We decree and declare that the enemies of debt, poverty, and lack have been handed over and will remain under our feet! *Not one word that our Heavenly Father has promised nor has any good thing that He has spoken—failed. All has come to pass for this ministry and our lives!* We are the seed of Abraham. All will see and acknowledge that we are the seed which the Lord has blessed.

We seal this powerful confession with the blood of Jesus and receive our budgets met, in Jesus' name. So be it. Amen.

Deuteronomy 8:18
Joshua 21:44, 45
Isaiah 48:17
Isaiah 61:9
Psalms 5:12
Psalms 35:27
Psalms 65:11
Amos 9:13–15
Matthew 6:33
John 16:13–15

CHAPTER

QUICK "ON THE GO" POWER CONFESSIONS FOR KINGS

This chapter is a quick reference point. If you just want to grab a quick snack this will be the place. Receive a quick dose of power by confessing what God says about you in His word. Speak confidently and boldly as you encourage yourself. You will be empowered tremendously, as well as your faith increased. Eat up!

> You shall also decide and decree a thing, and it shall be established for you; and the light (of God's favor) shall shine upon your ways.
>
> ~ *Job 22:28*

> So shall My word BE that goes forth out of My mouth: it shall not return to Me void (without producing any effect, useless), but it shall accomplish that which I please and purpose, and it shall prosper in the thing for which I sent it.
>
> ~ *Isaiah 55:11*

A. Call to Order

~ I take this opportunity to speak and declare divine order to my day and my night season! Anything and anyone misaligned (according to God's divine order), I call to divine alignment right now, in Jesus' name! The first fruit of my morning is holy and my entire day will be holy. I prophesy the perfect will of God to my day and night season so that my day and night season will know its place in my days. Divine order be! In Jesus' name. So be it.

~ I seek first the kingdom of God and His righteousness and all other things are being added to me!

~ I receive a fresh anointing to remove any burdens and destroy any yokes!

~ I commit to walk in the God kind of love this day and night season. I thank You Father for preparing hearts ahead of time to receive Your love through me!

~ I put on love. I enfold myself with the bond of perfection—which binds everything together completely in ideal harmony!

~ By the stripes of Jesus I have been healed. I am whole spirit, soul, and body!

~ The earth is filled with the knowledge of the glory of the Lord as the waters cover the sea!

~ I receive the grace of God to do all that God would have me to do in this day and night season!

~ My home is a haven of peace. My house is a house of prayer. I come against and cancel any division, strife, and or contention in Jesus' name! I declare nothing but victory!

B. God Inside Minded

~ I have the kingdom of God on the inside of me! I have peace, love, joy, righteousness and the Holy Spirit operating in and through me!

~ I receive Your voice God (directly) and the earth must obey me!

~ I receive Your voice God through the ministry of the Holy Spirit!

~ I love God's wisdom. I seek God's wisdom diligently!

~ I keep sound wisdom and discretion at all times!

~ I hear and I yield to the authority of God's word!

~ My mind may make plans, but it's The Lord Who is directing my every step and making them sure!

~ I recognize that the Lord my God He is God, the faithful God Who keeps His covenant, steadfast love, and mercy with those who love Him and keep His commandments to a thousand generations. I am the generation of the upright and I am blessed right now!

~ I allow the peace—the soul harmony—that comes from Christ to rule and act as an umpire (continually) in my heart. I am thankful, appreciative, and giving praise to God always!

~ I allow the word spoken by Christ to have its home in my heart and my mind. The words spoken by Christ lives in me richly!

~ Christ lives in my heart, through my faith. I am rooted and grounded in God's love!

~ I am filled with the fullness of God. I am fully flooded with God—Himself!

~ I am God inside minded. I really love The Lord. I keep and I obey His word, The Lord loves me and has come and made His home in me. I am the dwelling place for the Father, the Son, and the Holy Spirit!

~ I have high expectations in this day my Lord! I expect to experience Your love, Your presence, Your favor, Your grace, Your loving-kindness, Your goodness, and the impossible in this day and night season—in an unprecedented way!

~ I'm a king under the authority and influence of the King of kings and of the Lord of lords—my Lord and my Savior Jesus Christ!

~ As a king I rejoice in God! I bind myself by God's authority. I acknowledge His supremacy. I devote myself to His glory and His service alone. The mouth of those who speak lies against me will be stopped!

C. No More Sin Consciousness

~ I am born of God and I sin not! I am begotten of God, I keep myself and the wicked one cannot touch me! The devil has nothing on me!

~ I will never return to the vomit of the past!

~ I am no longer dominated by the world's spirit of error. The Spirit of Truth is leading me and guiding me into all truth. I am led by the Spirit of Truth!

~ I have dominion over sin. I am cleared from hidden and unconscious faults. I keep back from presumptuous sins and give them no dominion over my life. I am blameless, innocent, and clear of great transgression. I allow the words of my mouth and the meditation of my heart to be acceptable in God's sight. The Lord is my firm, impenetrable Rock and my Redeemer!

~ I consider myself dead to sin and I break any relation to it. I am alive to God. I live in unbroken fellowship with Him in Christ Jesus. I do not allow sin to rule as king in my mortal, perishable body! I am a king and I rule. I choose to keep my body under control. I do not yield to its cravings nor am I subject to its lust and evil passions. Sin no longer exerts dominion over me. I am not under the law as a slave. I am under God's grace, favor, and mercy!

~ I have been set free from sin. I now serve and yield my body to righteousness. I conform to God's divine will in thought, purpose, and action. I am dead to sin and alive to righteousness!

~ I do not belong to this world. I am no longer one with this world. I have been chosen and selected out of this world!

~ I am adorned in holiness. I have the beauty of holiness!

~ I refuse and I reject the natural inclination, preferences, and tendencies of fallen men!

D. The Holy Spirit

~ I receive the spirit of wisdom and understanding, the spirit of counsel and might, the spirit of knowledge, and of the fear of the Lord!

~ I choose life in every decision. I'm led by the Spirit of God and not by the dictates of my soul and my flesh!

~ I am not led by my intellect. I'm led by the Holy Spirit!

~ I am increasing in wisdom and in stature and in favor with God and man just like Jesus did!

~ I am in the Spirit. I hear the voice of God!

~ I live in the Spirit. I walk in the Spirit!

~ The spirit of wisdom and revelation in the knowledge of God operates in and through me!

~ I am filled with and controlled by the Holy Spirit!

~ The anointing of Jesus is evident in my life. I spend quality time in His presence. I seek His instruction. I hear His direction in all matters—in my heart and by the voice of the Holy Spirit!

E. More than Enough

~ The Blessing is upon me and my household! I expect favor! I expect monies found! I expect checks in the mail! I expect royalties! I expect bonuses! I expect raises! I expect the blessings to overtake me daily!—The Blessing is my lifestyle!

~ I can do all things through Christ Who strengthens me. I am self-sufficient in Christ sufficiency. My God has supplied my every need according to His riches and His glory (in and by) Christ Jesus my Lord!

~ The blessing of the Lord has truly made me rich and has added no toil or sorrow with it. My own works can not increase the blessing. I am already blessed!

~ I am the redeemed of the Lord! I have been redeemed from the curse of the law! I have been released from any cursed words spoken over my life! The Blessing of Abraham is upon me and my family!

~ I am the seed of Abraham. I am blessed with faithful Abraham. I am exceedingly fruitful—nations and kings come from me!

~ I am debt free and financially wealthy! I owe no man anything, but love! I am the lender and not the borrower! My faith is my currency!

~ I am blessed by God! I am fruitful. I am multiplying. I am filling the earth. I am subduing the earth. I walk in my God-given dominion and I am the blessed!

~ I receive, what is already done in the spirit realm. I cause manifestation right now by my confession of faith. I call those things to be as though they 'already' are!

~ I receive the increase of this earth!

~ Just like Jesus, I have the favor of God. All who see me will recognize that God is with me. Whatever my hand touches prospers. All that I set my heart and mind to is successful!

~ I meditate on God's word day and night. I am making my way prosperous. I am having good success!

~ By the grace of God, I do all things to the glory of God, and I am fruitful in every good work!

F. Increasing in Faith

~ I walk by faith and not by sight!

~ The voice of God is the stronghold of my faith!

~ My faith is rooted in hearing the voice of God! My faith is unshakeable!

~ I refuse to entertain doubt producing thoughts!

~ I am going from glory to glory!

~ My faith is increasing right now!

~ I am able to do nothing of myself, of my own accord. I am able to do what I see God my Father doing. For whatever the Father (God) does the Son does also. I am a son of God just like Jesus. I do not seek or consult my own will. I have no desire to do what is pleasing to myself (my own aim, my own purpose), but the will and pleasure of the Father Who sent me!

~ Whatever may be my task I work at it heartily, as something done for the Lord and not for men. Knowing with all certainty that it is from the Lord (not men) that I will receive my inheritance which is my real reward. Who I am actually serving is the Lord—Christ the Messiah!

~ I have a mouth, words, and wisdom that the enemy cannot gainsay, resist or contradict!

~ I boldly, courageously, and fearlessly proclaim and declare the name of Jesus!

~ The voice of the Lord says, who shall I send? And, who will go for Us? "Here I am Lord, send me!"

~ I am a letter from Christ. I am an epistle of Christ. The Spirit of the living God is in me and living through me! I am not sufficient of myself, but my power and ability and sufficiency are from God!

~ I have the God kind of faith. I speak to mountains (natural and spiritual) and they are removed! Whatever things I desire when I pray, I believe that I receive them and I have them!

Now to Him who is able to do exceedingly abundantly above all that we ask or think, according to the power that works in us, to Him be glory in the church by Christ Jesus to all generations, forever and ever. Amen.

~ *Ephesians 3:20–21 NKJV*

QUICK POWER CONFESSIONS FOR KINGS SCRIPTURES

A. Call to Order

Matthew 6:33
Isaiah 10:27
Colossians 3:14
1 Peter 2:24
Habakkuk 2:14

B. God Inside Minded

Proverbs 4
Proverbs 16:9
Deuteronomy 7:9
Colossians 3:15–16
John 14:23
Psalms 63:11

C. No More Sin Conscious

1 John 5:18
1 John 4:6
Psalms 19:12–14
Romans 6:11-12, 14
Romans 6:18–19
John 15:19
Psalms 96:9
Psalms 110:3
1 John 2:18

D. The Holy Spirit

Isaiah 11:2
Deuteronomy 30:19
Luke 2:52
Acts 4:8
Acts 4:13

E. More than Enough

Philippians 4:13, 19
Proverbs 10:22
Galatians 3:13–14
Genesis 1:28
2 Corinthians 4:18
Genesis 39:2
Joshua 1:8

F. Increasing in Faith

John 5:19, 30
Colossians 3:22–23
Luke 21:15
Isaiah 6:8
2 Corinthians 3:3–5
Mark 11:22–24

To order copies
of this book or to be placed on
our mailing list please email:

tlwpub@icloud.com

Books will also be made available at participating local bookstores and internet book distributors.

For more information or to contact
Tracy L. Williams, please write:

TLW Publications
P.O. Box 1413
Claremont, CA 91711

Tracy L. Williams

TheVoiceofTLW

Tracy L. Williams

Tracy

Or visit

TracyLWilliams.org